Special Praise for *May I Sit With You?*

"*May I Sit With You?* is heart-lifting and mind-opening. Tom's humility and simplicity are inspiring, sure signs that the words he shares come directly from his own practice. This is the sort of book to keep on your bedside table and open anytime you need to remember that mindfulness is possible."

Sharon Salzberg
Cofounder of the Insight Meditation Society
Author of *Real Happiness*

"A meditation book that finally incorporates meditation with a design for living. It felt as if my friend and colleague, Tom Catton, was sitting beside me, gracefully cheering my meditation practice on through the pages of *May I Sit With You?* The breath of this book brings every emotion, thought, or belief you have ever had into a meditation practice of healing and hope."

Sherry Gaba, LCSW
Psychotherapist and Life Coach
Author of *The Law of Sobriety*

"*May I Sit With You?* embodies the fruits of Tom Catton's meditation practice. It clearly comes from his willingness to be present to life with a deeply open heart. Tom's welcoming tone and rich, practical sharing are refreshing. This book generously opens an effective and inviting way to live the Eleventh Step. I highly recommend this book to anyone desiring to make a more conscious connection with their innate spiritual wholeness."

Rev. Anna Shouse, PhD
Unity Minister and Host of *Spirit of Recovery* on www.unityonlineradio.org

"Drawing from over forty years of personal experience, in *May I Sit With You?* Tom Catton skillfully invites his readers to cultivate their own spiritual path by providing a wide variety of accessible and gentle methods to develop a meditation practice of their own."

John (Chophel) Bruna
Director of the Way of Compassion Foundation
Dharma teacher and cofounder of the Mindful Life Program

"Tom Catton has a unique talent for distilling diverse spiritual teachings and practices down to their essence. *May I Sit With You?* is an irresistible invitation to share recovery, meditation, and the spiritual journey with a wise friend and steadfast companion. Full of great advice, clear guidance, and pithy teachings, this is a book to keep by your side and read again and again."

Kevin Griffin
Author of *One Breath at a Time: Buddhism and the Twelve Steps* and *Recovering Joy: A Mindful Life After Addiction*

"*May I Sit with You? A Simple Approach to Meditation* is a gem that introduces and expands on meditation and other mindfulness practices in an unpretentious, practical, and accessible manner. While the word *simple* in the subtitle may (and should) invite those new to mindfulness, Tom Catton's wisdom and experience shine through to enrich both novice and experienced practitioners of meditation.

"Each time I picked up this book, be it for minutes or for a more extended read, I left contemplative about the ongoing role of mindfulness in my life and with a reminder to be present for the here and now. *May I Sit With You?* is one of my favorite books on the topic and will be a go-to resource in my clinical practice for bibliotherapy and in-session readings.

"Accept Tom's invitation, and you will be grateful for it."

Dr. Lane Pederson
Author of *Dialectical Behavior Therapy: A Contemporary Guide for Practitioners*

"What comes to me immediately on reading this book is that I found it the most accessible and practical exposition and 'manual' on meditation practice of any I have yet read, and an inviting incentive to encourage us all to meditate. At once personal and playful, as well as profound and philosophical, Tom's natural flow of language is witty, whimsical, and wise all at once. His wonderful use of analogies, comparisons, contrasts, and distinctions brings to life each page and idea as he weaves together the twelve-step program with parallel Buddhist principles, with many other insights beyond those.

A sense of lightness and laughter, transparency, and authenticity flows through each small chapter. Tom captures the essence of why we want to sit together, finding peace, healing, and a sense of freshness of presence in life. His acceptance of all feelings and complexities encountered while meditating humanizes the process for us, removing a fear of failure and adding an anticipation of discovery. Clearly, this book and sitting is a 'path with heart' for the author, which he lovingly invites us to share."

Gay Leah Barfield, PhD, LMFT
Former Director, Carl Rogers Institute for Peace,
Center for Studies of the Person

"This inspiring book reminds us of the benefits of sitting still with the breath. The author offers us the opportunity to bring more joy and bliss into our lives by working with our difficulties and challenges, one breath at a time."

Valerie Mason-John
Coauthor of *Eight Step Recovery: Using the Buddha's Teachings to Overcome Addiction*

"*May I Sit With You?* is Tom Catton's complete blueprint for meditation in the purest form—being still, focusing on the breath, letting go of the past and future to be in the 'present moment, wonderful moment' and ultimately to become more intuitive and thoughtful in serving others. We are given an invitation to a more satisfying meditative experience and peaceful life—to be present, discover one's true self, serve others, and experience more love, joy, and connection. Please be good to you, and practice this gentle approach to continue your own adventure of self-realization."

Toni Tufo, MA
Former Spiritual Care Counselor at Betty Ford Center

MAY I SIT WITH YOU?

MAY I SIT WITH YOU?

A Simple Approach to Meditation

Tom Catton

CENTRAL RECOVERY PRESS
LAS VEGAS

Central Recovery Press (CRP) is committed to publishing exceptional materials addressing addiction treatment, recovery, and behavioral healthcare topics, including original and quality books, audio/visual communications, and web-based new media. Through a diverse selection of titles, we seek to contribute a broad range of unique resources for professionals, recovering individuals and their families, and the general public.

For more information, visit www.centralrecoverypress.com.

Publisher: Central Recovery Press
3321 N. Buffalo Drive
Las Vegas, NV 89129

20 19 18 17 16 15 1 2 3 4 5

ISBN: 978-1-937612-83-2 (paper)
978-1-937612-84-9 (e-book)

Photo of Tom Catton by Keith Kefford. Used with permission.

Publisher's Note: This book contains general information about addiction, addiction recovery, and related matters. The information is not medical advice and should not be treated as such. Central Recovery Press makes no representations or warranties in relation to the information in this book. If you have specific questions about any medical matter discussed in this book, you should consult your doctor or other professional healthcare provider. This book is not an alternative to medical advice from your doctor or other professional healthcare provider.

Our books represent the experiences and opinions of their authors only. Every effort has been made to ensure that events, institutions, and statistics presented in our books as facts are accurate and up-to-date. To protect their privacy, the names of some of the people, places, and institutions in this book have been changed.

Cover design and interior design and layout by Sara Streifel, Think Creative Design

To the spiritual warriors who continue to walk
a path filled with paradox and are called to
surrender again and again. To all sentient beings,
May you be free of suffering. May you be at peace.

TABLE OF CONTENTS

FOREWORD

In this book, Tom Catton has interwoven the liberation teachings of the Buddha with twelve-step recovery. A passionate practitioner of both traditions, he offers his deeply felt words and stories as an invitation to discover that freedom that is unconditioned by the particular circumstances of our lives.

It has been my good fortune and privilege to have known Tom for many years. Between the covers of this book you will come to know a man whose generous and compassionate heart has blessed many people. He does not talk about love; he writes from the ground of love that moves within him. He points to the transformative possibilities at the heart of Buddhism and twelve-step recovery.

This book is the product of an unfolding spiritual odyssey. It is a journey of inner discovery that will be of reassurance and inspiration to those wishing to embark on their own spiritual journey. I am grateful that Tom has documented his life in this heartfelt and deeply human way.

Gavin Harrison
Author of *Petals and Blood: Stories, Dharma & Poems of Ecstasy, Awakening & Annihilation* and *In the Lap of the Buddha*

ACKNOWLEDGMENTS

I must thank The All That Is, the joyful energy that created everything. I become overwhelmed with gratitude when I'm mindful that I'm a part of this cosmic dance. Thank you always to my beautiful wife, Bea, who is my dance partner and a constant reminder that all is perfect in its changing form. Thanks to the many people who touch my heart daily. Your friendship and support are appreciated.

I find myself constantly moved to write down the spiritual nonsense that streams through me. It's there when I wake up in the middle of the night, while sitting in meditation, while driving my car. I find myself scribbling it down at all hours of the day and night. This leads me to give special thanks to the several people who took each chapter I sent to them and literally crossed the T's and dotted the I's. Their talent made nonsense make sense.

Thank you so much to the publishing team at Central Recovery Press for allowing this second book to find its way to readers around the world. I love being a part of CRP; thank you.

INTRODUCTION

In the early 1930s, a hopeless alcoholic sought help from Dr. Carl Jung, a well-known Swiss psychiatrist. The patient had resigned himself to the tormented reality that he suffered from the chronic inability to stop drinking. In those days, such people often ended up in jail or a mental institution; many lost everything that had ever been dear to them, including family, friends, careers, and ultimately, life itself. Addiction was viewed as a lapse in morality and had not yet been recognized as a medical disease.

This man came to Dr. Jung and asked for help. The psychiatrist told him that although he was unable to help him, he had—on a few rare occasions—seen someone in the grips of alcoholism go through a profound personality change brought on by an intense spiritual experience. This visit, generated by a feeling of hopelessness, set into motion an accumulation of events that gave birth to the Twelve Steps. The twelve-step movement became one of the most powerful spiritual movements of the twentieth century.

What follows on the pages to come is about this profound personality change—an awakening of the spirit—and the importance of it happening again and again.

I attended my first twelve-step meeting in February of 1968 and have practiced the spiritual principles of this path, along with complete abstinence from alcohol or other drugs, since October 20, 1971. There are times when the spiritual path calls upon us to let go of old ideas, people, places, and things. This can make us feel like we have been stripped of everything that has given us a sense of being.

The devotion to living a spiritual life becomes a life of letting go, and one of practicing the spiritual principles for eternity. Yet the paradox is that we attempt to practice these principles moment to moment, day to day. The poet Emily Dickinson once wrote that "Forever—is composed of Nows." I believe this beautiful line is a prescient view of both the recovery and spiritual experiences. Even without our consent we seem to be led to surrender again and again; surrender becomes our offering to a world of impermanence.

I do not proclaim to be a meditation teacher, but it is with passion that I talk and write about the practice. I don't work in the field of addiction, nor am I a therapist, but I sponsor and work the Twelve Steps with men around the globe.

I'm a simple recovery guy with a passion to grow spiritually and share the spiritual path with others. Our Twelfth Step states that we have had a spiritual awakening and we are to carry the message to others. The message is, and always has been, the spiritual awakening that comes from working the steps.

Like the pursuit of education in any other school, my spiritual education has included many different classes and teachers. The difference is that there will be no graduation day; the call for continuing education credits is ceaseless.

The way of the Veda or Vedanta influence in the sixties captured the attention of my spirit while it permeated the philosophy that influenced the "flower children." I was immediately drawn to the words of Paramahansa Yogananda and Maharishi Mahesh Yogi;

little intellectual understanding was necessary, as the vibration of their words found their way to my heart. I suddenly knew what I wanted to be when I grew up: a spiritual seeker. Since then, there has been no turning back.

Over forty years later, my education continues with enthusiasm. I walk a spiritual path characterized by diversity, and my soul has been touched by a number of practitioners from many different spiritual paths.

The Twelve Steps act as solar lights that illuminate the path, guiding me in the right direction. Embracing the Eleventh Step enables me to fly freely in continuing my awakening.

My aspiration is to sit with each of you in silence and be mindful of our breath, knowing when we breathe in and breathe out, walking in the Pure Land of the beautiful moment.

This book contains no story line. You may open it to any page and begin reading. Each page contains a suggested message of contemplation and reflection for your practice.

You will find that meditation is full of repetition, and at times your practice will be nothing more than continually returning to the breath. This book is filled with repetition, and this is because our wandering minds need to hear the message, again and again.

CHAPTER ONE

THE EGO

The question is not "Why does ego constantly insult us?" but rather "Why do we listen?"

Ego, our lifetime companion, is the reason we will spend our tenure on Earth in spiritual practice. We can see when working the Twelve Steps that their intent is to rid ourselves of this adversary, cleverly disguising itself as a whisper from the divine.

Admittedly the efforts of ego should be applauded; it performs its assigned task with a vengeance, always in pursuit to avert our attention from our true nature. The vehicle it uses is the unobserved mind.

We experience thousands of uninvited thoughts per hour, accompanied by their sidekicks, emotions. Many people move through life feeling overwhelmed by emotions, as if an avalanche is pouring over them. They become stressed, depressed, sad, and angry—the list goes on. This process perpetuates the everlasting search for the hidden treasure, the secret key that will relieve these unwanted symptoms and subsequent feelings. We become convinced that more—more money, a more loving relationship, or a bigger house—will offer us relief. And of course, there is the obvious and ultimately damaging answer for many: a substance, something that will step in to tranquilize our emotional wounds. Ego will try to convince you that if you get what you're craving, you will be satisfied.

The real solace for me in this life, as it has been for many, was my introduction to the Twelve Steps, the superstar being Step Eleven. Through the practice of meditation I have learned to just sit and observe. I love the magic of my breath, which I feel by paying attention as I breathe in and breathe out. This practice also brings my awareness to uninvited thoughts as they arise. I'm able to sit and note their presence, while letting them travel on by as I say good-bye, repeatedly returning to the breath.

When we do not observe the nature of the mind, it's as if the mind has a mind of its own. Soon we are once again lost in our emotions. I'm confronted many times a day by obstacles that my thoughts try to convince me are real. But the practice of meditation acts as a translator to what is going on within. When feelings arise unobserved, they can take us captive. We become subject to anything they suggest, which may be anger, fear, or sadness. Going to our meditation cushion each morning, we can look forward to the practice of observing what arises. With a sudden awareness, we pinpoint why we are sad—the loss of a job, for example—but with clarity we see that many areas of our life are full of loving kindness. We can then let the sadness be with us, but it is not our whole life. We make friends with these uninvited guests, these emotions, learning to embrace them as they arise, bringing intimacy to the mystery of our mind.

My introduction to the twelve-step philosophy of "one day at a time" was a surprise awakening. It was a concept that freed my mind from thinking too far ahead, but twenty-four hours has now become a lifetime of thoughts. Meditation practice is about coming back to the present moment; even thinking of things in the near future can be the ego's attempt to open an unwanted doorway within.

I find that when grace snatches me out of the hands of ego and I remain present, I still cannot deny feeling "the presence." It's like landing in the lap of the divine. The joy and bliss that arise in that moment cannot be described with mere words. Is there more to enlightenment than being comforted in the moment? Maybe, maybe not.

While you practice meditation, I encourage you to sit through the restlessness, which is only the rhetoric of the ego. Restlessness is the ego's attempt to detour the seeker from sitting and touching his or her true nature. Countless times meditation practitioners have sat upon their meditation cushions and immediately experienced an explosion of thoughts. The goal of the practice is to disarm these thoughts. Our minds will unleash every distraction to convince us to stop meditating and busy ourselves with the nonsense of some unimportant task in a continued attempt to capture our attention.

It seems, at times, that the mind's sole purpose is to keep the practitioner distracted. A single inhalation and exhalation will introduce the silence of our own truth. The veil that separates us from our divine nature is so thin that it can be dispelled by the gentle breeze of breathing mindfully.

Simply put, the ego cannot survive in the moment. The practice of mindfulness is the invitation to the spiritual experience that will cause a profound personality change. This will result in the exhaustion and ultimate collapse of the ego.

CHAPTER TWO

A PLACE TO PRACTICE

The setting for your practice is important. When talking about my own Eleventh Step practice, I usually refer to myself as a bit "airy-fairy," by which I mean that my wife and I have a meditation room that is just for that purpose, a shrine-like environment decorated with artifacts we deem holy. You may find your favorite ambience in nature: sitting on the shore by the ocean or strolling through the woods and settling down by a stream to embrace your quiet surroundings.

Practiced meditators suggest that we create a spot to return to daily. I encourage you to explore this idea, whether the space is on your deck outside overlooking an expansive view, in a particular room in your house, or in a certain corner of a room. We can create a holy and inviting setting as long as we return daily. The continuous practice in the same space will effectuate the vibration of peace. You will find yourself wanting to continue with your practice as you approach your sitting area.

I find the early morning to be the best time to meditate. It is said that when the world around you starts waking up, its mental vibrations can be picked up. This is why 4:00 a.m. is a nice time to begin sitting, as most people in your neighborhood won't be awake yet. Sitting with one's own busy mind is enough to attend to, and when you bring in the sounds of the whole waking community, observing not only your thoughts but everyone else's will become an exhausting practice. I realize 4:00 a.m. may not be practical for everyone, so any time after you wake up but before starting your busy day would be desirable. The fact that you sit any time, rather than just thinking about it, will be of great benefit.

The ambiance my wife and I have created in our meditation room makes the early-morning call to practice one of ongoing enjoyment. I awaken between 3:00 a.m. and 4:00 a.m. almost every day. The ritual of practice begins as I walk downstairs and into the meditation room, which is already aglow with the inviting warmth of indirect lighting. My meditation cushion is in place before an altar; holy images of spiritual figures seem to gaze back at me. I sit between two large Tibetan singing bowls, and as I strike the bowls, their vibrations engulf the room; various crystals seem to catch the glow of candlelight. The fragrance of sandalwood incense in the huge brass holder fills my surroundings, and I find myself being transported to a singular place in my consciousness—my meditation has begun. This doesn't happen automatically. It was established by a daily practice that has existed for decades. In my experience, the excitement to sit each day in a space that was created for Eleventh Step practice is enticing and effective.

CHAPTER THREE

THE PRACTICE

I always assure people that I don't care how they practice Step Eleven, either by prayer or by meditation. The technique will probably vary over the years, but the key elements are discipline and passion for the practice. I have been meditating on a regular basis since 1966 and have been initiated into many different forms of practice. For the past twenty years I have been practicing mindfulness; I'm drawn to the school of Theravada Buddhism, from where the now-popular Vipassana, or insight meditation, originated. You will find the word *mindfulness* is used throughout this book. It is the technique of following the breath to remain present. Mindfulness comes from the Sanskrit words *sati*, which translates to "basic awareness," and *smirti*, which means "to come back" to awareness when the mind starts to stray. Simply put it means "Pay attention to what is."

Mindfulness is an intentional, nonjudgmental awareness of remaining in the present moment. Acceptance of what life offers in each moment becomes a prayer. We sit with awareness and observe what arises. We don't try to fix or change our experience; instead we let life become both the student and the teacher and allow each moment to become our lesson plan.

The common way to practice mindfulness (Vipassana) is to begin by finding a comfortable position that will keep the spine straight. Some people will cross their legs or sit in a lotus position; others find a meditation bench beneficial. Regardless of the technique or seated position, you want to be careful to not cut off or inhibit circulation. If you sit in a chair, be sure your feet are flat on the floor, or if outside, flat on the ground. I use a meditation bench. It's as though I'm kneeling, but I'm sitting on a low bench with my legs tucked under me. In this position, the pressure is not on my legs.

Breathe normally and follow the breath as it enters through the nostrils. It might be a cool or warm sensation, or you might sense a rising and falling of the chest or belly. Just follow the sensation of the moment as you breathe in and breathe out. The practice is to consciously breathe. You might notice that you are thinking. Just note, *I am thinking,* and gently return to the breath. We do this again and again. The goal is not to stop intruding thoughts but to observe them and not get attached. Everyone who meditates, from the beginner to the devotee of twenty or more years, has thoughts. It is what we do with each thought that counts. Our purpose for meditating is to stay present, so even when noises or other distractions occur, we can use them to remind us that we are present.

When we hear noises, they remind us to gently return to the breath. As we notice the activity of the mind, we embrace the effortlessness of our breath as it gradually guides us back to the present. Vipassana also teaches us to scan the sensations of the body from the head to the feet, focusing our attention on each area, noting which sensory phenomena are rising and falling. If there is pain or some other sensation in one particular area of the body, we embrace the feeling rather than try to resist or change it. If for some reason we have to move, we do it gently and remain aware of our adjusted position.

The practice of meditation invites us to participate in nondoing. Meditation isn't about doing nothing; it's about doing nothing else. The purpose isn't to stop the thoughts and feelings that appear or to manipulate them to bring about joy or bliss. We are requested to sit and observe and not attach to the mind's (ego's) splendid array of distractions, determined to kidnap us from the moment. When we are assaulted by thousands of thoughts, the exit strategy is to gently return to the breath. This conscious act is done again and again. This is the practice. When practicing moment-to-moment awareness, we may be surprised to see how short-lived each thought actually is.

Distractions are a part of everyone's meditation, not just the beginner's. It's normal for our first thoughts to seem like a nuisance, but we soon realize that these distractions are what it's all about. Our lesson is to learn to deal with these distractions without dwelling on them. Learning to deal with a simple thought and watching it disappear is our training for those times when life hurls another challenge our way. Like watching a thought, our practice is to detach; soon it will pass away.

We soon see that this becomes the ebb and flow of life. Thoughts come and thoughts go; challenges come and go as well. The rhythm of life becomes the same dance: Life comes together, and life falls apart. Our lesson is always to observe and not to become preoccupied by following the never-ending story line.

Being mindful of our life force is our introduction to enlightenment. We summon mindfulness to follow us throughout our busy day. We move away from nondoing to doing, recommitting to our intention of paying attention from deep within and purposely observing even the most mundane movements. By witnessing life, rather than attaching to each event, each thought, we gracefully respond to each challenge in lieu of "reacting."

Showing up each day to our area of practice, sitting and paying attention to our breath, even for ten minutes, reinforces our discipline to start our day with mindfulness. When breathing in, we know we are breathing in; when breathing out, we know we are breathing out. This simple task, repeated again and again, can change our lives.

Our practice becomes one of remaining open to the ongoing challenges and obstacles that seem to throw themselves at us. This open-mindedness becomes the path to the divine and to our inner joy; the divine plan was in place before our arrival. Difficulties can now guide our spirit to finally awaken.

We find peace when we embrace and accept the gifts and demands of life, now that we are equipped with our practice, returning to the moment again and again—always coming back to the breath. When thoughts slow down, the eyes of the spirit open, and we see the world through the eyes of an alert, yet humble, sage.

CHAPTER FOUR

RESTLESSNESS

"I can't sit still long enough to meditate" is a common response when the practice is suggested. The Thai dharma teacher Ajahn Chah once observed that some people thought that the longer one sits, the wiser one must be. However, true wisdom comes from being mindful in all postures. I gently explain to men I sponsor that there are twenty-four hours in each day; however, if you can't devote the morning to extended meditation, please sit for ten minutes and be mindful of your breath. The mind will wander, but keep returning back to the breath. Keep returning again and again to the breath.

Restlessness is common in the practice of meditation. In Theravada Buddhism it is considered one of the five hindrances, or obstacles, to sitting meditation. I experience its appearance not only in my daily practice upon rising, but also when sitting on a retreat. I have been on many three- to ten-day retreats. After I arrive and check in, I'm confronted with the fact that I'm there without my normal distractions, and then the mind games begin. A multitude of thoughts drop by for their uninvited visit, trying to convince me that I have to leave. This onslaught of restlessness can last a few hours or even for the first day or two.

Whether it happens during a ten-day retreat or a morning meditation of twenty minutes, our only defense is to allow the restlessness to arise and to acknowledge it. When allowing any feeling or thought to arise, we are being present with it. This immediately brings us back to the moment. The truth is that we can't be present and feel restless at the same time. We breathe in and breathe out. Suddenly the restlessness dissolves into peace. The invasion of thoughts is drowned out by the roar of silence as we become lost and then cradled in the moment. The projection of the impossibility of sitting for ten minutes can turn into thirty minutes of just being present.

To become lost in the moment is to be lost in love. The only way this happens is to sit through what our ego will continue to assault us with—intrusive thoughts, determined to trip us on the spiritual path. With steadfastness we stay with the breath and suddenly stumble in the moment; the paradox is then revealed. Becoming lost in the moment is always a gift.

The practice of mindfulness encourages us to think only of this moment. It introduces us to the space called *here* and the time called *now*. We meet each moment exactly as it is. In this way we can become intimate with all that arises within. The phenomenon of being present is the result of sitting through the restlessness and purposely paying attention to what life offers in each moment.

CHAPTER FIVE

GUIDANCE

As we travel across our beautiful planet, we are guided by signs posted on the roadways that indicate where we are and how to get where we're going. For more information, we refer to a map. Since roads and pathways have true directions, wouldn't our spiritual path also have true directions?

The practice of meditation, encouraged in Step Eleven, serves as our signpost and map as we travel the spiritual path. Access to these directions will assure us that we're in the right place at the right time. Anyone who is a true seeker has a lot of "baggage"—after all, we are on a spiritual journey! The information you find within you when practicing sitting meditation tells you what to carry and what to discard.

Be mindful as you follow your breath. While breathing in, *pay attention to breathing in*. While breathing out, *pay attention to breathing out*. Observe your thoughts as they float by. In this simple act of practicing the presence—not attaching to any of our thoughts—we can become receptive to the whisper of the universe. We can always find the inspiration that leads us closer to our soul's purpose.

In my study of mindful meditation, I haven't discovered a lot written about the guidance we can find in our practice. My motivation for exploring this phenomenon is my interest in Buddhist recovery. I realize the Buddha's teachings are primarily concerned with suffering and following the path to end that suffering. Buddha wasn't a big "God guy"; in fact, contained within the Buddhist mythology is a story where Buddha chastises Brahma, the Hindu deva (god) of creation, for returning beings to the cycle of birth and rebirth. Yet regardless of Buddhism's views toward any belief in a supreme being, so many people attracted to Buddhist recovery have no problem with the word *God*. They're not insinuating that there is a guy with a long white beard directing our lives. "God" is just another way of speaking of the force of love that connects all things.

Throughout the past forty years, I have practiced the art of mindful listening in my meditation. My previous book, *The Mindful Addict*, is full of stories documenting many adventures ignited by guidance I discovered while listening within. Yes, most of the time it is *monkey mind*. Monkey mind is a Buddhist term meaning "unsettled; restless; whimsical; inconstant; confused; indecisive; uncontrollable." The monkey jumps through the trees from one branch to the next; this is a metaphor for our thoughts as our mind jumps from one thought to the next. So when it is not monkey mind, it is important to follow your heart.

I ask any Buddhist who is not fully convinced about guidance or thinks it sounds too much like theism and the supreme-being gig to think about the Buddha as he sat under the tree and experienced his miraculous awakening. When he came up with the Four Noble Truths, where did they come from? Was this inspiration he received? I think so. And I call that *divine guidance*.

CHAPTER SIX

IMPERMANENCE

The divine comedy is that everything the ego entices us with is impermanent. The ego plays its part, convincing us and promising us great joy and fulfillment—if only we acquire a big bank account, a perfect marriage, a nice home, new cars, and more things. Impermanence is one of the many spiritual principles I embrace while working the Twelve Steps. As I move through my life I call on this principle many times, especially when my heart is broken by my unrealistic attachments.

In the act of observing what is, we learn the impermanence of thoughts and feelings that arise. By sitting and not attaching, we learn to wave goodbye to them. In experiencing the simple feeling of wanting to scratch the itch at the tip of our nose, but not doing so, we learn that by just noting the feeling, it soon disappears. Small lessons such as these soon advance us to larger challenges that appear in life. We find from experience that when we just be with all that is going on around us, without following our stories to a fantasized outcome, our feelings will change as we move on to the next moment. Life is always in transition. The only constant in life is change.

Embracing impermanence opens a door to our true nature. A feeling of bliss and joy can arise from deep within us for no apparent reason. In this awakening, we realize that true joy has always been who we are, and that all the outer things we cling to, such as people, places, and things, have always been impermanent. Clinging to the material world can only produce a temporary happiness that leads to despair as our outer world changes.

We must also be conscious that even clinging to the idea of enlightenment is another parlor trick of the ego. Enlightenment is also like our lives: an unfurling process of experiences rather than a target we place in the crosshairs of our ever-desirous ego.

When the principle of impermanence becomes embedded deep within, the spiritual seeker notes the tribulations that have been caused by reaching for outer circumstances in seeking greater fulfillment. This clinging ultimately ends with joy, contentment, and security slipping from our grasp. The spiritual path leads us all to times of being stripped of almost everything. To experience impermanence at this level is a sort of baptism, which alone drives one to practice, knowing the path to lasting joy is moving through life with mindfulness.

In Tibetan Buddhism, they have a ritual that honors impermanence. Several monks work on a sand painting that consists of different-colored grains of sand. They create beautiful mandalas, certainly works of art. Some can take weeks to create, with many monks working simultaneously. When the mandala is finished and enjoyed by others, they sweep it clean, destroying it completely. This is done to demonstrate impermanence.

Change makes all things possible. We hear it reinforced throughout the recovery programs that it is not change that causes pain, but rather our resistance to it. Whether we are addicts or not, we soon realize that we seem to be universally addicted to struggle and resistance. That is why surrender is the key that unlocks every path toward change in our lives, regardless of tradition, religion, lineage, or life philosophy. Suffering would never end if things didn't change. The phrase *This too shall pass* hangs on the walls of many recovery meeting rooms throughout the world. The law of impermanence persuades and affects all things in life to change.

CHAPTER SEVEN

EQUANIMITY

Equanimity has become my compass to guide me through life's array of challenges. It protects me from my own denial system when I want to avoid unpleasant feelings and circumstances. It teaches me to accept praise and rejection equally, with the same attitude of gratitude. Equanimity enables me to observe and embrace anything that is in my life, and to do so without judgment, simply because it's in my life.

When I had about thirteen years in recovery, I went through a divorce, and the pain of the separation broke my heart wide open. This, of course, turned out to be a gift. I started working the Twelve Steps again with a passion I hadn't experienced before. The steps seemed more important and revealing than my first time working them. I found myself opening the door to life like never before. Somehow I knew I had to let go of judgment of whom I would let into my life and whom I wouldn't. Everyone and everything became important. I began to let in whatever and whomever appeared.

My new mantra became "Maybe, maybe not." The Christian mystic St. Francis of Assisi compelled us all to "wear the world as a loose garment, which touches us in a few places and there lightly." Wearing life more loosely, in order to keep things simple as they appeared in my life, I became interested in seeing what was to be offered.

The dharma (teachings of the Buddha) has given us equanimity as our defense against suffering. All situations become opportunities to grow spiritually when attended to without judgment or labeling them as "good" or "bad."

CHAPTER EIGHT

PAY ATTENTION

Most of us can recall these two words; we've been hearing them from the time we could first understand language. When we reflect back to early childhood and throughout our school days, this spoken phrase stands out. It is also a favorite of the military; the command to "Attention!" is sounded off many times a day.

I had no idea I was being called to spiritual practice in my early childhood. Surely my parents, teachers, and commanding officer had no idea they were uttering words that would be so significant in meditation practice.

Meditation is essentially sustained concentration, and if practiced, it gives us the ability to walk peacefully amid the adversities of life—just by paying attention. Mindfulness is practicing the art of paying attention to what is. Mindfulness seems to be a gentler way of saying "pay attention." Being present for our every moment is an exercise we can all do. No experience necessary. On-the-job training provided. Start now!

I saw a segment on CNN that said we have become a nation on medication. Let's become a nation on meditation. Let us become spiritual warriors and help ourselves and others to practice what we have been called on to do since childhood: pay attention and be mindful.

I greet the early-morning darkness with a yawn and, focusing only on the sacredness of the moment, I prepare myself for practice. When you wake each day, even without a regular meditation practice, take a few breaths with the sole intention of paying attention. Try a ten-minute practice. With twenty-four hours in each day, taking this short time to sit and be mindful of your breath can be a game changer.

The simplicity of breathing in and being with that breath, then breathing out and knowing you are doing so, is the portal into the present moment. Let the breath become a personal mantra; when your attention is on the breath, you are being present.

While heart rate is a constant presence of the human life, it can deceive us in moments of fear or doubt as our blood flow increases and adrenaline surges through our bodies. Yet we can control our breathing; coming back to the moment naturally calms us, allowing the heart to follow our breath into the moment of now. Be mindful, as the next breath could contain the greatest joy you have ever experienced.

The practice of mindfulness brings great significance to the most mundane actions. The simple walk from one room to another, done with complete attention, can be like surfing a perfect wave. The present moment contains everything we are seeking. Practicing presence with all we do opens the door to joy, and being truly present for others is an offer of humble holiness and service. We are of service to others by giving our personal attention to each individual we encounter on our journey through life.

The occupation of mindfulness has my complete attention. For all those who practice, it is job security for a lifetime. Each moment we begin anew, returning to the breath, to the moment we are involved in now.

"When the flower blooms, the bees come uninvited" was one of many realizations by the nineteenth-century Hindu mystic Sri Ramakrishna. Our own blossoming occurs in meditation, and we experience peace as we begin to unfold like Ramakrishna's proverbial flower. The simplicity of paying attention to our breath finds its way into all areas of life. Practicing mindfulness turns our daily routines into both a sacred and practical path; we find magic while embracing each moment and each other. The next time someone says "Pay attention," let it be your reminder to become mindful of the present, beautiful moment.

CHAPTER NINE

SIDE EFFECTS

Television shows are inundated with advertisements promoting some new drug or other to combat illness of the body or mind. Commercials show people waltzing through green fields, basking in sunlight, smiling, and enjoying their new lease on life because of yet another magic pill. These ads are followed by the warning of menacing side effects, such as diarrhea, sleepiness, sexual dysfunction, restlessness, and depression that may even cause suicidal thoughts—oh, and be sure not to drive heavy equipment.

The viewer must consider if the harmful side effects outweigh any potential benefits. And, of course, there is the ever-present fine print at the bottom of the screen that is too small and too lengthy to read, and appears for too few seconds to comprehend. Yes, at certain times and in certain circumstances, some people need to take medication. But I wonder how many aches and pains and even illnesses could be eliminated or reduced if simple meditation were prescribed rather than an arsenal of medications.

I don't *recommend that you stop taking any medications without first consulting with your doctor or medical provider.*

I *do* recommend that you let your doctor know that you meditate or are considering it, and explain the benefits of doing so. Practitioners of Western medicine do good work; science has given them many tools to treat the sick or injured. Maybe your medical provider will share your insights about meditation with others. *Another opportunity for you to serve others.*

Since the late sixties and early seventies, meditation's ability to help with stress reduction has been explored. The scientific community's research has proven that this simple, daily practice can improve one's overall health and quality of living. Meditation had its coming-out party on the world stage in the 1960s with the book *Autobiography of a Yogi*. This book and The Beatles' visit to Maharishi's ashram in India gave Transcendental Meditation (TM) its wider exposure and its vehicle to spread through the United States.

One of the first studies on the physiology of meditation was the dissertation of UCLA graduate student Robert Keith Wallace. In 1970, part of this study was published in a science magazine. Since then Dr. Wallace has contributed to the increasing body of research into the physical benefits of meditation and consciousness.

Jon Kabat-Zinn, also a pioneer in the study of the benefits of meditation, has helped spearhead a movement that utilizes mindfulness meditation for stress reduction. His methods go back to the late 1970s after he attended a meditation retreat led by Thich Nhat Hahn and began to realize the benefits of meditation for both mental and physical health. Today many HMOs offer meditation groups for patients to learn how to relax into a healthier body.

In 2006, researchers at Harvard, Yale, and MIT released a study on the effects of Vipassana, or mindfulness meditation, on the human brain. They discovered that experienced meditators actually had improved brain function, improved attention, and improved ability to process thought.

Like the medications advertised on television, the practice of meditation may also cause side effects. Some of these may include the following: recognizing love in everything; feeling deep compassion for all sentient beings; experiencing spontaneous joy; being at peace in the moment; wanting only to serve others; listening to the guidance of a still-small voice within; seeing light with eyes closed; having an urge to dance when no one else can hear the music; knowing great peace while moving through a difficult challenge; and generally acting as a fool while playing your part in the cosmic show. These "side effects" sound a lot less harmful than the pharmaceutical side effects we are familiar with from the television ads!

As I said previously, *do not stop any medications without checking with your doctor first.* But don't the side effects of meditation sound wonderful?

The practice of Step Eleven is fundamental for the awakening of our spirit, but the ancient practice of meditation is finding its way into the medical and therapeutic communities. And, as mentioned above, research continues to document the physical and mental health benefits of meditation and can be found in numerous scientific journals. Visiting your meditation cushion more frequently could result in improved health and well-being. Excuse me, may I sit with you?

Thoughts That Encourage Enlightenment

Anticipation is a path to the future.
If I step upon it, I'm no longer present.

Practicing the presence is job security for a lifetime.

It was a hot, sunny day. As I bent over to take a drink from a garden hose, the warm sun embracing my shirtless body and the cool water running down my throat and spilling out on my bare feet, a joy suddenly swept over me. I found myself crying uncontrollably—experiencing the simplicity of being caught in the moment.

While breathing in, know you're breathing in.
While breathing out, know you're breathing out.
This simple practice can transform lives.

Expectations are the footlights on the path to suffering; acceptance is a guiding light on the path to peace.

Whether an emotional, physical, or other type of roadblock is encountered on our path, we can embrace it, and it can act as a slingshot toward the divine.

Daily and with great intention, return to your inner life.

The path our heart follows is determined by what motivates us. When you awaken each morning, ask yourself, "What can I do for someone else?" This is love put into action, the glue holding the universe together.

The inner drive for perfection is a step on a path that can only lead to pain. Mindfulness will transport us to the sacred path of recovery.

Embracing our imperfections, we give birth to our spirituality.

The simplicity of "lightening up" will spawn our enlightenment.

There are no dharma or meditation police. Your practice is your practice. The way you work your program is the way you work it. Blame becomes obsolete.

The truth that can set us free is simple: What we put into life in this moment determines the next moment.

The material is the spiritual made visible. Everything is light vibrating, and all things have a resonating tone. Listening deeply, we can hear the music emanating from all objects; going even deeper into the silence, we hear the universe singing the primordial sound, *OM*.

When Darshan turns into Shakti,
you'll know if it happens.

The next breath you take will
be filled with joy, so pay attention.

The best way to fulfill one's karma is to live the dharma.

It's not that complicated: Just be here now.

Mindful listening is when all sounds
become the chant of a monk.

Bliss is a notable experience, but like any, it is not one to
become attached to. Just observe, *I'm in bliss.*

There is a fine line between having expectations and
holding great intentions and positive thoughts for things
to come. The first surely leads to suffering.

Falling into grace? *Okay, I'm always open to that.*

Never defend the joy you feel or your gratitude for life.
Even while experiencing some great challenges,
you have been touched by Spirit.

Something I embrace in this sometimes
crazy world is good karma and grace.

Suchness, a term used in Zen, signifies the welcoming of accepting what is. With suchness, all ordinary moments become magical and blissful.

Back by popular demand, The Now; enjoy it!

Take a moment now and say with loving intention, "Send someone to interfere in my life." You have now set events in motion to have a beautiful day.

Speak the truth; listen deeply;
trust emergence; it's practice.

When practicing mindful listening, you listen not only with your ears but also with your heart.

To know and understand the nature of your mind, you must observe it.

My most memorable travels have been not by plane or train, by bus or car, but rather in meditation when I have journeyed within.

The practice of mindfulness will influence you physically, mentally, and spiritually; living in The Now is living in harmony.

Catch your next breath, and I will meet you within.

Practice mindful smiling as you move through your day; it will serve others.

It is easy to live in a state of waiting for what we *hope* will bring us fulfillment, but it takes practice to embrace what is right *now*.

If we all practiced meditation, we would hear the whisper of our soul's purpose, and it would sound like this: *Serve others*. This awareness would generate a tidal wave of gratitude across our planet.

Pure contact with the moment is a direct path for encountering enlightenment.

Experience something so beautiful, profound, and magical that no degree, no guru, no secret sect is required. Simply practice *being* in the present moment.

People become beautiful . . . life experiences transform . . . colors feel vibrant . . . songs seem to be sung by angels . . . joy ripples within; but only when I pay attention.

When you observe that you're not present, you have just arrived back in The Now.

When I note worry and fear in my life, it is a sign that I'm in the future. When guilt or sadness prevails, I'm living in the past. Both motivate me to return to the wonderful moment, beautiful moment. Let's breathe together now.

If I'm looking at the past for my identity and
looking toward the future for my fulfillment,
then the path always ends in suffering.

Surrender is our willingness to be present with what is.
Surrender is our introduction to equanimity.

It's a beautiful moment when we emerge from
forgetfulness and return to the wonderful breath.
Bring immediacy to your practice.

Holding on to the intention that the universe
is *for* me and not *against* me has a striking effect.
Life becomes groovy.

Intelligence is marvelous. Nonetheless, there will
be times when only our heart has the answer.

There is no way to escape the moment;
eventually we have to disconnect from our distractions,
dive within, and sit with what arises.

CHAPTER TEN

HAPPINESS

Each morning, sitting upon my meditation cushion, I'm greeted by a sign with a quote credited to Pierre Teilhard de Chardin, the progressive Christian contemplative and philosopher. It expresses the sentiment that joy was an infallible sign of God's presence. Teilhard de Chardin was a fascinating, if not complex, figure and spiritual teacher whose teachings are worth exploring. But every day that I look at the sign in my meditation area, I am reminded of this simple truth: The quest for joy and happiness is natural; we just seem to look in all the wrong places.

My previous book, *The Mindful Addict*, was written with the intention of showing others that the practice of a spiritual path will bring both guidance and happiness to our lives. This happiness is born from within, rather than from any outer influence and condition.

Our practice is challenged each day. We hear about or experience incidents that invade our lives, which seem to throw insults and obstacles toward any attempts to find happiness. There is a blunt-yet-popular saying that tries to assure us: "Life is hard, and then you die." This statement is somewhat true, yet I refuse to embrace this as my worldview of life in general, let alone adopt it as my mantra.

Our practice is to return to the simplicity of the present moment. We find shelter from the intrusion of malevolent thoughts by surrendering to our benevolence within. The goal of the spiritual practice is to soften, not harden, our lives. Ultimately, we must change how we view our life and our inevitable death. We realize the need to accept things peacefully, allowing all situations, good or bad, to act as a catalyst for our continued change. We learn to respond to praise or rejection with an attitude of gratitude. This is equanimity.

The practice of meditation—coupled with service to others—will not assure a gold star will be placed next to our name. Challenges will continue to confront us, but returning to the practice again and again with the willingness to start over will have a softening effect on our daily lives. We realize that we are not victims and prisoners of this life after all, but rather participants in our own moment-to-moment liberation.

Why all the talk about the Eleventh Step as it relates to the practice of meditation?

Why do I write about it, speak to others about it, and practice it?

I'm convinced that there is nowhere else to find true refuge in this world; the practice transforms my world into a hermitage, and my daily routine becomes a retreat. Meditation demands nothing of me but my full attention, and that is a small price to pay for the infinite peace it brings to my life.

I read essays and books on this subject from many eloquent writers, mostly meditation teachers; some possess letters signifying various degrees and titles that follow their names. The essays and books may discuss the subject of meditation from varying perspectives and viewpoints. However, the conclusion, for me, is always the same.

There must be something to this meditation thing.

I have no formal education, but I have practiced meditation for over forty years. I can't debate or have an intellectual conversation on the complex structure or comparative nature of world religions. I can't explain the different levels of consciousness that occur during the enlightenment journey—but the simplicity of showing up each day and sitting upon the meditation cushion is available to all of us; no degree is necessary.

My life, like all human lives, has had its share of disappointments, and it can seem impossible at times. I experience deep pain and loss. I like to call this "living life to the fullest." In the midst of profound change, I return to the sanctuary of the wonderful moment and eventually touch the great joy within. I owe this to my practice. Happiness is a state of grace I experience most of the time, regardless of whether I am supplied with what I "think" that I need.

The happiness you feel through enlightenment is not something you might experience in some lifetime to come. It is attainable in the next breath, as you sit and then serve others. The only fee required is to pay attention.

CHAPTER ELEVEN

ENLIGHTENMENT

Chop wood, carry water. What is the sound of one hand clapping? The long-sought-after experience of enlightenment among seekers is at times considered out of reach, attainable by only the disciplined sages of the Far East.

In my early studies, I assumed that only years of practice, consisting of hours of meditation each day, or even an inevitable expedition to the peaks of the Himalayas penetrating the ashram of a wizened or withering guru, were the ways to capture this elusive experience. I discovered a different truth altogether as I began to actually practice meditation. Enlightenment is available to everyone.

I do a daily practice of meditation as part of my working Step Eleven. It doesn't include sitting upon a meditation cushion praying for enlightenment. Rather, I sit and observe what arises, always returning to my breath. This simple act of coming back to the moment again, and then again, is my practice. The doorway to enlightenment is not the entrance to a cave, but the simplicity of being in and staying in the moment. Enlightenment is not a mirage, nor is it a game show that we somehow "win." Enlightenment is a life choice, if not a vocation.

Anyone who has experienced joy or bliss arising from within, for no worldly reason, can attest to the fact that they had no power in manipulating this experience. This is where the paradox comes into play. It is suggested to meditate every day, and yet we are told to expect nothing, that even this actual craving for enlightenment can cause more separation and greater suffering. We just sit and observe thoughts, paying attention to the sensations that arise, placing no labels or expectations on them.

The experience Bill W. (the founder of AA) had in his hospital room seemed to come out of nowhere. There were no days of extended meditation that preceded this event. When Eckhart Tolle, author of *The Power of Now*, awoke and was suddenly struck by enlightenment, he found himself sitting on park benches with feelings of bliss for the next two years. These experiences seem more like a gift than something people can consciously orchestrate in their lives. These examples of enlightenment are as personal as they are universal. Anecdotes such as these are proof positive that miracles are real because they forever alter the life of the recipient.

Enlightenment can seem like a random awakening, a strangely delivered gift. And those who are truly enlightened seem equally gracious in sharing how they came into contact with this experience. So it seems that enlightenment is based not on selfish evolution, but rather on a clarion call sent out to those who will listen.

There's an abundance of spiritual books describing enlightenment and transcendental states of consciousness; some recount different levels the soul must experience to obtain complete freedom. Such writings often leave the reader longing for an experience that seems to be kept behind lock and key, forever hidden in some mystery school or discipline practiced in a far-off land.

When grace snatches me out of the hands of ego, and I find myself present, I cannot deny feeling grace's presence. It's like landing in the lap of the divine. The joy and bliss that arise in that moment cannot be described with mere words. Is there more to enlightenment than being caught up in the moment? Maybe, maybe not.

After forty-plus years of practice, I'm drawn to the simplicity of being present; I will remain open to the possibility that there is more. Perhaps my patience is an indication that I have glimpsed enlightenment. My duty now is to continue the practice and help shine a light for others to see.

Living each moment of the day with mindfulness is the switch that, when flipped, awakens the spirit, preparing us for enlightenment, which can come at any moment. We never know when enlightenment will strike. But it seems that it is a reality, and we must be in the present moment to receive its life-altering grace.

CHAPTER TWELVE

METTA PRACTICE

Metta is the practice of sending loving kindness to oneself and others. It teaches us a deep compassion for life. Being mindful of loving kindness can promote forgiveness to those it is directed toward. In the teachings of the Buddha, metta is a form of prayer; just as you are directed to pray for others, sending loving kindness creates the same container (conditions) to work within.

I have always been told when praying for self or others to follow it with the words *Thy will be done*. This neutralizes the request and carries with it the acknowledgment that I may not know what is good for others or even myself. When sending out metta, we always start with the word *may*: *May I experience a life of love* or *May others experience joy within*. The use of the word *may* takes the demand out of the request, thus becoming the neutralizer.

Metta can be your whole meditation practice. It differs from mindfulness, where we observe thoughts that arise and continually return to our breath. Sending out loving kindness is an action-based meditation. When I lead a meditation sitting, I let people know that I will ring the bell to signal the group that the remaining minutes will be spent practicing metta. I find that ending my meditation in this way provides a lovely balance to my practice.

When on retreat, you may find yourself practicing many times a day, for many days in a row. Some retreats have walking meditation times; this physicality, combined with mindfulness, breaks up the practice of sitting all day on the meditation cushion. Bringing metta into your meditative practice can help feelings that arise from long periods of sitting. Feelings about life situations can and do arise; we can feel our hearts empty out. Feelings of despondency can appear, and we can use metta to send loving kindness, for example, "May my heart be filled with love and compassion," or "May I be led to right understanding of what is."

When sitting upon the meditation cushion for long periods, we may send love to our cramped legs and aching bodies. Our egos can tell us that if we don't move and stretch we will never walk again, but by sending love and appreciation to our body temple we can work through our physical pains. We see and then experience the sensations of the impermanence of our thoughts.

Metta and prayer are both essential principles that should be called upon with routine frequency as we move through a life that seems to lash out at us with chaos and doubt. To watch the news in today's world will bring tears to the eyes of many, sometimes followed by feelings of powerlessness to reach out and help so many in need. Practicing metta teaches us to embrace compassion; we learn to put love into action, with opportunities arriving in each moment.

There are many ways to be of service to a life that is starved, sometimes by giving money, sometimes by giving your time, but always by silently sending out loving kindness to the hearts of others. Close your eyes now. Someone in your life needs compassion; maybe it's you. Silently project the words *May love be felt within the heart*.

CHAPTER THIRTEEN

PRACTICE RADICALLY

Just as entering the twelve-step arena can ruin the "enjoyment" of using, practicing mindfulness meditation can "ruin" living in the past or the future. The daily practice of Step Eleven can eventually become our most important moment of the day. The goal is to carry those moments of mindfulness with us as we arise from our meditation and carry on with our daily responsibilities to ourselves and to others. Noticing our breath throughout the day, we find ourselves refreshed as we return to conscious breathing. Being mindful of our life force is our introduction to enlightenment.

Showing up each day to our area of practice to sit and pay attention to our breath, if only for five to ten minutes, forms our discipline to begin our day with mindfulness. When breathing in, we know we are breathing in. When breathing out, we know we are breathing out. This simple task, repeated again and again throughout the day, can change our lives.

We discover that not all recovery or support group meetings are vibrant and inspiring, but we "keep coming back." Like support group meetings, not all meditations present us with easily recognized gifts. Many times the message we receive is riddled with thoughts, bombarding us with more questions than answers, and at times returning to the breath is almost forgotten; yet we keep coming back each day. We don't have to understand the experience of what is going on by showing up to sit upon our meditation cushions, but we continue each day, again and again.

When does a conservative practice like mindfulness meditation become radical? Let's reflect on why some of us ended up in a twelve-step program with years of recovery behind us. The answer is simple: The using and acting out no longer worked. We were left with the realization that drugs and alcohol, or whatever else, would not give us the relief that they once promised. Only then could our denial be seen initially and eventually overcome.

With the daily practice of mindfulness meditation, we learn to observe and understand our minds. We learn to watch the thoughts that enter and leave our minds. We learn to sit and just *be* with the emotions that rise and fall in response to these thoughts. We merely observe and don't attach; when we find ourselves lost in the wilderness of our thoughts, we immediately return to the sanctuary of our breath. When we are not in the moment, that realization acts as a slingshot, propelling us instantly back to the wonderful moment. This is how we practice radically.

CHAPTER FOURTEEN

COMPASSION OR CODEPENDENCY?

There's a fine line between compassion and codependency. Both are ignited from witnessing the suffering of others, especially within the immediate family, or someone else. In most cases, where suffering touches the life of those with whom we are personally involved, codependency appears disguised as compassion.

If the suffering is caused by addiction, the immediate fear may be losing our loved one to the disease. With codependency as our driving force to help alleviate the suffering of another, we can quickly cross the invisible line of trying to save the person and doing anything and everything to change their circumstance. We fall into the trap of thinking that we can control the outcome, becoming convinced that somehow, some way, we can manipulate the outcome and save someone from their own destructive behavior. We do everything we can to buffer the pain of everyone involved, but what we are really doing is saving the person from facing the consequences of his or her addiction.

We may get mad and disgusted at times, but we still continue to give more money or excuses. These actions give the message to others that if they keep using, we will always be there to support them, even if it kills us. In the end, our attempts to "help" or "save" them are really our desire to control a situation that we have no control over. Wish them well, then let go. You can't fix them.

When we are confronted with the suffering of others, it can act as a kind of catalyst to our own spiritual practice. When this happens, it can be the turning point where codependency starts leaning toward true compassion.

Following the admission that we can't always manipulate a favorable outcome, we come face-to-face with our despair and hopelessness. This awareness can also be a turning point and bring about the birth of compassion toward our suffering and that of others. Through the spiritual practice of a daily meditation, our codependency is transformed into compassion. Our heart opens wide and our love for others and for ourselves becomes unconditional.

Turn on the television to any news channel, and you will be inundated with the suffering of so many people on our planet. Since we are so far removed from these tragedies, our distance from the calamity easily becomes a buffer shielding our heart. We can see it and hear about it, but not really *feel it* within. We practice letting our hearts become wide-open as we witness the wars and poverty that seem to blanket so much of our world. We allow this suffering to touch us deeply within, and we embrace our tears as they start to flow. We must lean toward what we fear. We can't show compassion toward others until we learn to show compassion for our own lives and touch our own suffering by letting our own hearts burst wide open to the divinity that surrounds us always.

CHAPTER FIFTEEN

NINETY SITS IN NINETY DAYS

Members of twelve-step recovery groups have heard the words "ninety meetings in ninety days" spoken in meetings throughout the world. This challenge to the newcomer is made not only to establish the discipline of attending meetings, but also to allow them to reap the benefits of doing so. The nature of our mind, when controlled by ego, is to fill our heads with self-talk that convinces us that to show up for anything that would benefit our lives is unnecessary.

A stream of thoughts, containing an infinite amount of convincing excuses as to why we *can't* show up, often flows from our twisted thinking. These messages are not the true message from the divine, but originate instead from within the ego that does not want to go into retirement. The ego leads us astray from our true destiny. Meditation keeps us present in the moment and keeps the ego at bay.

I would like to suggest to devotees of the Eleventh Step to meditate on the advice of the slogan "ninety in ninety"; use it as the inspiration to practice meditation daily. The busy and restless mind will endeavor to put its most convincing voice to your ear. "I'm too busy" or "I have to leave for work early," and so forth, are messages the ego will try to use to prevent you from starting your day with mindfulness. Our commitment to practice is our initiation into the realm of the spiritual warrior. With this new status, we win over the false self with kindness and love.

Show up daily, sit on your meditation cushion, and you will experience paradise by breathing in and breathing out mindfully. Mindfulness turns all experiences into a prayer. You will be roused within to seek a deeper practice.

CHAPTER SIXTEEN

THE FOUR NOBLE TRUTHS

The Buddha's teachings are centered on the Four Noble Truths.

1. Life means suffering. (**Step One**. We admit our powerlessness.)
2. The origin of suffering is attachment. (**Step Two**. We came to believe in the cause of our suffering and insanity.)
3. The cessation of suffering is attainable. (**Step Three**. Freedom from addiction is attainable.)
4. The path to the cessation of suffering is the Eightfold Path. This is where admission, belief, and thought end. This Fourth Noble Truth is the Eightfold Path. (**Step Four through Step Twelve** of the Twelve Steps are contained in the Eightfold Path.) These are the action steps, where we take inventory, share it with another, strive to be a better person, right our wrongs to the extent possible (**Steps Four through Nine**), and stay on the path of self-improvement (**Steps Ten through Twelve**).

Acknowledging the Four Noble Truths and the effort some of us expend in working the Twelve Steps have the same goals. These goals are as follows:

1. *Right View.* This means to see and understand things as they are. Suddenly, a spotlight is pointing the way to the Four Noble Truths and the Twelve Steps illuminating our path and allowing us to see clearly. In recovery this process starts with our inventory. By writing out our emotional life story, we begin to see that we are not alone as we begin to understand the law of karma: that we aren't being punished and that we set the ball rolling.

2. *Right Intention.* When working the Twelve Steps and embracing the principles contained within them, we begin to commit to self-improvement. Right intention is what inspires us to show up for practice each day. It brings us back to our breath when lost in our story line. Our intentions turn in a positive direction, we look for ways of serving others, and we begin to develop compassion for suffering in the world around us.

3. *Right Speech.* This principle might seem obvious, but in reflection we can see how our words have hurt others. Wars among nations have been started by mere words. Tell the truth when communicating, and be mindful not to gossip. We soon want to embrace kindness when speaking with others; some of us might even want to talk less.

4. *Right Action.* Our actions are important as we move through life. We want to abstain from many things: harming any sentient being, taking the life of another, taking what is rightfully not ours, engaging in sexual misconduct. Our actions are the energy source and building blocks that

create our karma, the law of cause and effect. What we put out eventually comes back.

5. *Right Livelihood.* How we make our money is important. Like right actions, it can have a great effect on our karma. We want to stay away from occupations that in any way harm others or our planet. It is highly recommended that we stay away from the distribution of alcohol and drugs both in the spirit of twelve-step recovery and in the principle of right livelihood. Also engaging in prostitution, selling weapons, and working in the industry of slaughtering animals for our food are not recommended. This is why many people become vegetarians. We can be against the slaughtering of animals, but if we are eating the meat, that act is something to consider.

6. *Right Effort.* This can be applied to all the principles contained in the Eightfold Path and the Twelve Steps, for it takes effort to practice them in our everyday lives and to live in harmony with those around us.

7. *Right Mindfulness.* This principle calls for us to be a part of life as it is happening. Mindfulness is one of the most important and talked-about principles in the process of ending suffering. The practice of mindfulness brings our attention to the present moment; the breath is considered the vehicle to The Now. This is one of the most talked about and practiced of the Buddha's teachings. Getting a glimpse of this concept, we realize it has always been about The Now.

8. *Right Concentration.* This principle is based in the act of concentrating on positive thoughts that encourage enlightenment. While practicing mindfulness, we focus

our concentration on the inhalation and exhalation of our breath; this takes great practice. Our concentration will develop as we continue to show up daily. Mindfulness and concentration walk hand in hand as we participate in our daily practice.

The Four Noble Truths and the Twelve Steps are in alignment with each other. Both contain principles that will produce an awakening if those principles are applied to our lives.

CHAPTER SEVENTEEN

MINDFUL WALKING

When attending a retreat, the daily schedule usually includes sitting meditation, teachings, and walking meditation. The discipline of showing up for meditation each day is to encourage our practice of mindfulness to follow us throughout the day. Learning to walk with mindfulness is our first lesson in allowing our practice to continue after we rise from the meditation cushion.

Like breathing, walking is one of the things we do without much conscious effort involved. We usually seem to hurry through our day almost running to each new task, moving forward unconsciously. Learning the technique of mindful walking is another way of being present in the moment.

Being on retreat is a wonderful time to learn walking meditation. When we arrive, we leave our distractions at the door. Our time on retreat is like becoming a monk or nun. All of our needs are met. We just show up and learn to sit, letting our thoughts and feelings arise. While practicing walking meditation, we walk with no destination or purpose in mind. We walk to walk. We slow our pace down, for there is nowhere we need to be and no certain time to arrive there. As we move, we note each step. We feel the floor or the earth we walk upon. Our steps become aligned with our breath. Feeling the breeze on our face, letting any sound come to us, we are chasing after nothing, and we are simply walking.

When we are walking with the intention to pay attention, everything in our view comes alive. Colors become more vibrant. Suddenly, we feel connected with our environment as we move slowly and mindfully. Looking down upon the grass, we see the sunlight reflected upon each blade. The slight movement of air caused by our passing gently moves each shimmering blade as though it is waving to us, thanking us for noticing its simple and natural beauty.

Retreats are wonderful times to enhance our practice of sitting and walking meditations. When returning to our hurried life, we will release stress by continuing our daily practice of sitting and being mindful of our natural movements throughout our day. Keeping our focus on the moment, we use our mindful walking, along with our breath, to keep returning to the wonderful peaceful moment. A simple way to practice is to pay attention as we walk to the next room in our home, when we finish with our regular sitting meditation. We feel the carpet or the hard floor under our feet as we move from room to room. As we leave the house and walk to the car, we simply practice walking to the car.

The more we practice doing what we are doing, while we are doing it, the more ordinary movements throughout our busy day become extraordinary. Life becomes poetry in motion, and feels like a series of yoga postures, one followed by the next. The breath of life takes on new meaning when we consciously, deliberately breathe. With the intent to pay attention to the most mundane tasks, each moment becomes the best and most joyous moment of our lives.

CHAPTER EIGHTEEN

HINDSIGHT

The continued practice of meditation teaches us to stay in the present. Ongoing practice reminds us to neither project into the future nor dwell in the past. In my spiritual practice, hindsight has become an important principle that I call upon often. I use what I refer to as *right view* when practicing hindsight. I'm revisiting some past experience rather than dwelling on it. I visit, I learn, and I come back to the moment. I don't stay there trying to relive the past, allowing the movie to play over and over again in my mind while expecting a different ending.

When confronted with the many uninvited challenges that life offers us, we can find ourselves in the midst of yet another story line. Story lines are usually created by "all or nothing" thinking. We experience a stampede of thoughts; always it seems the worst-case scenario leads the charge.

When we can call on right view, we begin to step back and observe the latest drama we are involved in. With hindsight, we revisit some similar challenge from our past. Suddenly we are able to see with our spiritual eyes that the universe has always been on our side. We see with 20/20 vision that each moment unfolded as it should. With grace, we see that this obstacle is really an oddly wrapped gift.

Hindsight helps keep our hearts open and vulnerable in each moment and allows us to see things in the same way that the sages see them. We reach for our principles in a time of need. We have come to believe that a spiritual transformation is always the way to a moment of peace.

Hindsight can be invaluable to anyone struggling to understand the "why" of their suffering. Someone may ask, "Why did this happen to me?" As we gaze back at challenges we have been through, we see the pathways that led to the true outcome, not the roller-coaster ride our story lines had us caught up in.

Thoughts to Contemplate

The next time you find yourself feeling bored or contemplating your purpose here on Earth, try focusing on the moment and the breath you are experiencing. That should keep you busy for the remainder of your life.

Conscious breathing is the doorway to the moment. The sacred art of mindful breathing eliminates our preoccupation with the pain of the past and the anxieties of the future. Please practice daily.

If you feel that hole in your gut, then become whole through your practice. This will bring you back to the moment. When we are wholly focused on the present moment, that moment becomes holy.

I'm on a path that calls for continuous surrender. Starting over again and again is the practice. Just breathe.

Living the dharma, accepting our karma, staying away from the drama, that is our purpose. Don't take any of it seriously. It's all impermanent.

Be here now in this present moment—
this wonderful moment.

Once you taste the joy of the present moment, living a life of mindfulness becomes your primary goal.

It is said that our only prayer should be for knowledge of His will for us. If you do pray, let the words you utter in silence be these: *Send someone to interfere in my life*. There is no greater reason we are here than to serve others.

There will be many times along our path when certain hurdles seem impossible to get over or through. It is like being stripped of everything that is dear to you, left with nothing to hang on to but your sorrow and pain. We sit with our surrender until hindsight clears our vision, and then we see that the universe has bestowed great love and grace upon us. Things change—even our perspective.

Sitting within the silence this morning, I became mindful of your great pain. In the stillness before dawn, I was given right view. I saw within the mind's eye your old self dying, clutching to hang on to power. As this process took place, your heart was being stretched to new boundaries so that more love, compassion, and joy could be yours. This process may hurt now, but be still and know great things lie ahead.

As we travel our path, people will come and go; some will stay for a lifetime, some for an instant. We may experience connections or none at all. Energy is exchanged at a heart level; we may be touched deeply, or our presence may touch another deeply. By being mindful with all whom we meet, we can be assured we will not miss a beautiful encounter.

Never lose your wonder for life;
embrace the magic in each moment.

When applying the principles of impermanence and equanimity to life's ups and downs, to the suffering and happiness, we find that we seem to be viewing it all through the eyes of a sage. We find that all that remains is absolute joy.

As I am sitting in the predawn, with a halo surrounding the candlelight and the aroma of sandalwood filling the room, my breathing slows down, almost undetectably. The sound of silence awakens me with its roar, *OM.* Then grace comes upon me and my heart touches joy. I'm flooded with light and give thanks. Then I go wash the dishes.

Describe the spiritual life in one word: *paradoxes.*

Be mindful. The next breath could contain
the greatest joy you have ever experienced.
Put nothing ahead of your practice.

There is a calling for people who have discovered true happiness in spite of outer conditions, and this is to teach by example the art of mindful living. Not only are we clean or abstinent from our old harmful habits, but we can live life from a place of deep joy. Pass it on.

I think we're on to something . . .
present moment, beautiful moment.

I think living simply so others may
simply live is a groovy idea.

When mentioning meditation, a vision of sitting on a cushion in silence comes to mind, but when moving through life with mindfulness, all actions become meditation. Dancing, running, riding your bike, driving your car, washing dishes, or making love—the act isn't important. Being present in your life is; it is a great gift. Keep practicing.

Let yourself be swept within by the next breath. Begin to live in the here and now. Great happiness and love will become your motivation to serve all sentient beings.

I had a dream in which I took a pen and wrote the word *God* on the showerhead. It felt like I was bathing in holy water. Strange, but I assume this was safer than when I waded in the Ganges River.

While waiting for an encore of a pleasurable experience from the past, we miss the simplicity of being present and touching the joy of now.

Before we proclaim to know someone intimately, we must deliberately spend time observing the nature of our own mind.

Who we really are is obvious, but the mind creates a delusion; this is why it is so obviously missed. Deep practice dissolves the delusion.

To cultivate compassion, breathe *in* the suffering of all sentient beings, and breathe *out* loving kindness.

I'm a devotee of this moment, not the last and not the next.

Learn to speak fluently the language of the heart; it is universally understood.

The first excuse when suggested a daily practice of meditation is "I don't have time." A simple fix is to get up earlier.

A list of what it should be like if you are free is what undermines your freedom.

We can count our blessings for the good fortune that the universe is kind enough not to manifest all the drama imagined by our wandering minds.

To hear angels sing, listen to the silence;
to be lost in love, serve others.

Don't try to figure out the mystery of the breath;
just observe.

My thoughts today were *No more sleeping or eating; just sit in meditation*. I shared this with my wife, who is an excellent psychologist. It was decided quickly that I'm nuts.

Memories and anticipation are trapdoors used by our ego, causing us to fall through and out of the moment.

Knowing that you seek an "awakening of spirit" causes my heart to leap with joy.

Eating natural foods, sleep, and exercise are spiritual practices when you realize the divine uses your body temple to announce itself to the world.

While meditating, I found myself lost in beautiful thoughts, but thoughts nonetheless. At least ten minutes had elapsed and, noting this familiar phenomenon, I immediately returned to my breath. The impact was glorious. I was immersed in the sound of silence and peace, and it was like the prodigal son returning home. The Now was always there; I'm the one who wandered off.

Addiction drives us to revisit that which torments us.

When embarking on the journey within, pack lightly.

I remember sitting on a boulder two days' hike out of Pokhara, Nepal. The dawn has broken, revealing a spacious view of the snow-capped Himalayas. My gaze falls on the dharma-colored robes of a monk, who slowly and with intention approaches me. As he passes close by, our hands go to the prayer position, and with the same breath we speak the greeting of Namaste. My heart is touched with joy.

Meditation practice invites us to do one of the simplest and yet one of the most difficult tasks: to sit still and be present.

CHAPTER NINETEEN

PARADOX

If your life at times is full of confusion and paradox, I say, "Welcome to the spiritual path." Shariputra was one of Buddha's principal disciples and was questioning Avalokiteshvara, who is the bodhisattva of compassion, about his confusion with a certain practice. Avalokiteshvara answered with the most famous of Buddhist paradoxes: "Form is emptiness; emptiness is also form. Emptiness is no other than form; form is no other than emptiness."

The more we practice meditation and living in the moment, the more we seem to be confronted with paradox. One simple definition of a paradox is that it is a situation of two opposite forces occupying the same space; what seems impossible is now not only possible but also true. So on a deeper level, paradox could really be viewed as a miracle. Paradoxes confuse the ego. While it's distracted, trying to figure things out, we learn to rest in what the moment offers us. A recovery mantra and spiritual truth I believe is: *Surrender to win!*

Surrender is the flashpoint of both spirituality and recovery; by "giving up" and "giving in" we are actually relieved of the heavy burden of ego. In twelve-step programs, this paradox of "surrendering to win" has saved countless lives and continues to do so today.

Love has the potential to open the heart and then the mind. Suffering has the potential to open the mind and then the heart. Both are needed on one's spiritual quest. The practice of meditation is the vehicle we use to go within. Although we learn to just sit in practice, expecting nothing and embracing what arises and falls, our destination subtly becomes our true nature, the homeland of joy.

The more we awaken and connect with joy, the more we begin to mature spiritually, as our eyes and heart open to the suffering of the world around us. Only then can we begin to serve others. Only then can our joy lead us to compassion.

Through meditation, the paradox of suffering and joy become apparent. The more we wake up, the more we are called upon to touch the suffering around us. People in twelve-step programs know this all too well. We cannot recover from our addiction unless we stay in the trenches with those still addicted and suffering.

The bodhisattva—one who has awakened—vows to take rebirth after rebirth in order to help all sentient beings awaken. This is a beautiful example of someone who has awakened to the love of the universe and, instead of just resting in this light and love, has chosen to feel and heal the grief of so many.

There was a time early on in my meditation practice when I first stepped onto my spiritual path and thought that if I practiced meditation and service to others I would never hurt again. This is certainly a vision of someone new to the spiritual life. I have realized now after decades of spiritual practice that my spiritual growth was out of my hands. I have seen on many occasions how the universe directed me in ways that at the time I didn't understand; only years later did I understand that it was the fastest way home.

The joy in our lives can inspire us, it can ignite the fire within, and sometimes it may even feel as though we will explode with this love and joy bubbling up from within. We learn to embrace the suffering or grief when it returns; we let it open our hearts for others, and let it soften the moment. With each awakening, we are given the potential to experience the love that is the cohesive force for the universe; yet in attempting to be environmentally conscious and help the planet, we are also given the potential to experience the suffering. Don't try to shield yourself from suffering. It goes hand in hand with true joy.

If life seems to be full of paradoxes and contradictions, don't be alarmed: You have stepped upon a path that leads to many wonderful things.

CHAPTER TWENTY

THE FIVE HINDRANCES

Twenty-five hundred years ago, Siddhartha (Buddha) spoke about how he had been seeking enlightenment for several years. He came upon a huge banyan tree and seated himself under it with a vow to find liberation in the face of the forces that cause suffering to all sentient beings. While sitting, he was confronted with the five main hindrances by Mara (ego). These were desire, aversion, sloth, restlessness, and doubt.

When we practice meditation, it's quite common to be approached by one or more of these hindrances at any given moment. In the simplest terms, these hindrances are sent to us from the ego. During meditation, the ego's main purpose is to delay our inevitable union with our true nature. Most of our thoughts distracting us during meditation originate from one of these hindrances. We have been taught in the practice of mindfulness to observe our thoughts, sit with them, and rest with things as they are. As long as we don't attach to our thoughts, they will dissolve. This is the law of impermanence, a principle that we encounter on the experiential level during mindfulness meditation.

Desire in this case is any longing that focuses on one or more of the five senses for happiness and pleasure: sight, sound, smell, taste, and physical feeling. This is the type of desire that can lead to addiction: always reaching outside of ourselves for something to alter our mood, to stop the pain, or to feel pleasure. Later I will discuss the desire to know God and deepen one's spiritual life, how this desire can be a motivation for the discipline it takes to show up daily for practice.

Aversion is our avoidance of or attempt to push away negative or painful thoughts, such as anger, resentment, and hostility. One of the goals of meditation is to learn to embrace what life offers, to learn to observe what arises, explore it, embrace it, and let it move on naturally.

Sloth is when we find ourselves with heaviness of body or dullness of mind. You may have a tendency to want to fall asleep during meditation when caught up in this hindrance.

Restlessness is when our minds are agitated and unable to settle down. I addressed restlessness earlier in Chapter Four and consider this to be the one hindrance that discourages and even prevents most people from meditative practice. If you can't settle down and even start to meditate, you won't be there, sitting, long enough to experience any of the other four hindrances, or the gift of watching them dissolve as you sit in practice.

Doubt is when we feel like we will never be able to understand or implement the instructions about meditation. If we are practicing with a teacher, we might start to disbelieve the teacher or his or her teachings. Most people in twelve-step recovery have certainly experienced doubt. We come into the recovery program with feelings of not being enough and of feeling "less than." This feeling exists among people whether or not they are in recovery.

We can overcome these hindrances in the same way that Siddhartha did, while sitting in meditation. Even in the midst of being assaulted by our own minds, we keep our hearts open and just watch our thoughts as they pass. As long as we don't attach or avoid these transient feelings and thoughts, we can find a quiet place to rest in the chaos of our minds. Suddenly, we will touch the peace of our true nature and find ourselves awakening with each breath. *Buddha* means "One who is awake." May you live with ease.

CHAPTER TWENTY-ONE

TONGLEN

In January of 2006, I was in a severe automobile accident and fell into unconsciousness. I had a CAT scan at the emergency room that showed no signs of head injury. As time passed, though, I started having terrible headaches and many other symptoms that indicated something was wrong. After two months, the doctor decided to do an MRI, which showed my brain had been bleeding during that entire time.

It was during this two-month period that I was led to the meditation technique of tonglen. Our seemingly primal and innate tendency is to avoid pain at any cost. With tonglen meditation, we invite pain within; it becomes our guest. Whatever unpleasant situation you might be experiencing, you can sit in meditation and consciously breathe it in. With intention, you *breathe in* the pain of other sentient beings who may also be feeling the same anguish that you are experiencing. You then *breathe out* loving kindness to those who may be afflicted with the same challenge. This practice is a unique circular form of healing that can help transform your pain into compassion for others.

I would show up for my meditation practice every day. I would begin my meditation as I always do. I just sat and was mindful of my breath. After sitting for fifteen to twenty minutes and observing the many thoughts that tried to capture my attention, I would begin to focus my attention toward my headache with the intention to breathe in the pain. I would consciously think of others who might be going through pain from bodily injury, and then attempt to breathe in their pain, too. Holding this in my heart, while I tried to emanate loving kindness (metta), I would then breathe out and send this wave of healing to those who were also in severe pain.

Tonglen can be practiced for any emotional or physical pain. Any time you sit for this practice, you can be assured that there are many throughout the world who suffer and feel as if they have no hope for relief. Our willingness to take on their pain and help to heal them creates great compassion for their very suffering. It gives your pain a purpose: We drop any thought of *Why me?*

We turn our pain into a vehicle to touch others deeply. In the simplicity of sitting in meditation and practicing tonglen, you are sharing your heart with many around the planet. This is an amazing way to be of service to others without even leaving your meditation cushion.

Immediately after my MRI, I was rushed up to the neurology department. The surgeon who read my MRI met me in the waiting room and asked how I got there. He said, "We have to admit you right now. After what you experienced during the accident, you shouldn't even be alive, or at best be able to even walk or talk." The surgeon then explained that my brain was completely pushed over to the right side of my skull. In hindsight, I am certain that the reason I was functioning at all was from the two months of practicing tonglen meditation every morning. In my attempts to send out healing energy to others, I was somehow healing myself as well. This is perhaps another paradox of being of service. As we try to help others, we invariably help ourselves.

In my case, one could argue that the practice of tonglen literally saved my life.

CHAPTER TWENTY-TWO

RETREATS

Retreats are certainly something to consider for anyone with a sincere practice of meditation. I'm certainly not suggesting that one must spend years in a cave in the Himalayas to gain enlightenment. Retreats come in an assortment of sizes and formats, from one day to three months. When I say "retreat," it is in the context of an organized gathering with a retreat leader or meditation teacher. Many people make excuses that there isn't enough time to participate in a retreat. Even a daily practice, doing morning meditation, finds many citing the lack of time as an excuse. The truth is that the busier we are, the more important it is to meditate on a daily basis.

There are many one-day retreats available where forty-five minutes to an hour of sitting is followed by teachings, and then participants sit again in silence. This type of retreat also usually involves mindful walking as a form of the meditation. My wife and I both have attended many retreats, from one day to ten days. I have found them all beneficial. I believe that creating a space, empty of mindless chatter, while having extended periods of meditation, punctuated by spiritual teachings and even discussions led by the retreat leader, is such a boost to our overall spiritual development.

Most retreats require silence, no eye contact with others, no books, and no writing materials. Even the one-day retreats are practiced in what is commonly referred to as "noble silence." However, when teaching is in session, questions may then be asked by attendees.

The goal of any meditation retreat is to deepen our practice of entering into the silence. Books, pens, and paper are distractions from this process, and attendees are usually asked to not bring these items to the retreat. I have found longer retreats give me space to finally slow down and become comfortable. Removing oneself from daily activities sets the stage for spiritual connection.

After three days at a retreat, a settling-in period seems to take over. Our "busy self" finally surrenders and gives up. Over the years in my practice of meditation, I have learned that showing up and expecting nothing is the key. The simplicity of following my breath, noting my thoughts and body sensations, isn't always easy. Expecting guidance, desiring to see the third eye, wanting a bright light, or yearning for any type of transcendental experience just causes more attachment and suffering. We can be distracted by our own ideas and misconceptions about our personal journey. Even our previous positive experiences of past meditations or retreats can actually inhibit our growth, as we cling to our expectations. The recurring lesson is to sit, listen, and experience what comes up, again and again. When we get caught up in the false enchantment of our minds, we break the spell by returning to our breath. Quite simply, this is the practice of mindfulness meditation.

CHAPTER TWENTY-THREE

THE BREATH

When we practice mindfulness meditation, the instructions are to follow our breath. If we are mindful of our breath, we are primarily in the moment. Through the practice of being present, we move through life with much less stress and drama.

Many forms of meditation also contain a mantra, a word or a phrase repeated again and again. Some might stare into a candle or at a picture of someone they deem to be holy. All of these methods are based on the practice of samadhi, or concentration. Whatever we choose to enhance and utilize in our practice should be geared toward the ultimate goal of mindfulness. We should be able to have our chosen technique with us at any given moment. It is my belief that one certainly shouldn't feel obligated to spend a large sum of money to achieve the benefits of meditation. The breath seems to fit this description.

Our breath is continuous, automatic, and free. These three criteria can be the doorway to mindfully surrendering to this very moment. Breathing is so simple that most of the time we aren't even aware we are doing it. We take no thought in performing this life-giving process. Meditation calls on us to be conscious of something we are already doing. Everyone on the planet is breathing—all races, the rich and the poor. There is no sacred initiation to go through to breathe. We just have to practice every day in order to become mindful of the breath as we inhale and exhale. Our heartbeat can be influenced by things from our environment, such as hearing loud sounds, or from interior emotions, which can send our hearts racing as adrenaline rushes through our bodies and minds.

We are powerless over this universal physiological phenomenon. However, during times of stress or confusion in our meditation, we can control our breathing. We pause, take a few deep breaths followed by calm exhalations, and return to the practice. This is another benefit of using the breath as our vehicle for meditation practice.

Breathing is always happening in every moment, whether we are paying attention to it or not. Each mindful breath touches our true nature; we receive the gift of awakening our enlightened minds. The breath becomes our refuge in the midst of the chaos that can circle around us. It can immediately pull us back to the moment when our thoughts have us traveling to an unhappy destination over some real or imagined challenge.

Breath meditation is letting the body breathe in a natural way. Barring the aforementioned moments when we feel as if we must take a few deep breaths to return to our meditation, we are not practicing any kind of forced or rigid breathing as suggested in some breathing exercises. Mindfulness is not so much a breathing exercise as an attempt to return to the present moment. Our breath becomes a guide and friend who leads us back to this place, the eternal now, again and again. It is a gentle process that we don't have to think about, but we do want to watch it and pay attention to it.

Mindfulness meditation practice is not the only meditation that involves the breath. During my time spent studying and practicing the teachings of Paramahansa Yogananda, I went through three years of training in Kriya Yoga, culminating in mindful breathing directed at a certain area of the body. In Kriya Yoga, the technique involves one full inhalation and one full exhalation where you direct the breath to a certain area. The goal of this practice is to be with the breath during the entire cycle of the technique.

"The Holy Breath" is a common phrase heard in the Christian realm. In many of the Vedanta (Hindu-based) practices, the breath is an important part of the meditation. In chapter six of the *Bhagavad-Gita*, Lord Krishna describes what might be the first recorded instructions on meditation. What he teaches is, in essence, breath-guided meditation. In their translation of the *Upanishads* (like the Gita, another key text of Vedanta), Swami Prabhavananda and Frederick Manchester described these ancient teachings as the "Breath of the Eternal." The idea of *breath consciousness* is a central thread that seems to run through the collective tapestry of all surviving religions and wisdom traditions.

The practice of mindfulness breathing is something that can easily be carried with you throughout the day. In fact, this is the goal of mindfulness: not only to just be present while sitting on your meditation cushion, but also to practice the presence throughout the entire day. The twenty minutes we sit in practice each day exists to prepare us for the remaining hours of our day. It's always the last thing I do at night. Once I turn off the lights, I instantly embrace my breath as I make the transition to sleep.

CHAPTER TWENTY-FOUR

THE SOUND OF THE TIBETAN BOWL

When on a retreat or sitting within a meditation group, it is quite common to observe a Tibetan singing bowl sitting beside the teacher or the person leading the meditation. When the bowl is struck, the beautiful sound resonates from within. It's this sound that calls us to mindfulness.

These bowls are traditionally made of a special seven-metal alloy of gold, silver, iron, mercury, tin, copper, and lead. The bowls are tuned to our seven musical notes of A, B, C, D, E, F, and G; each note is aligned with one of the seven chakras.

The singing bowls are used in meditation and sound healing. We know that sound is a vibration, and although we can't see it, this energy wave has a great effect on our brain waves and spiritual bodies. Our normal waking state of consciousness during our daily activities is called the Beta state. When we are awake and relaxed doing light meditation, we move into the Alpha state of consciousness. When we practice a deeper meditation, we experience the Theta state. The deepest is the Delta state, which can be found in a deep sleep or very profound states of meditation.

The sound vibration of the singing bowls enables people to be quickly transported into the realm of these subtle brain waves. A twenty-minute experience with the bowls can take someone into a state of meditation that might require them to otherwise participate in a retreat for several days to experience. I have been providing Tibetan bowl treatments since 2009 and have had the pleasure of witnessing people go into deep states of consciousness by surrendering to the vibrations within. You can purchase CDs or sound files featuring the recorded sounds of the bowls, but to lie down on the floor and feel the vibration, as well as hear the sound, is an enlightening and singular experience. Many have walked out of my meditation room after returning to the normal waking Beta state and have shared their impressions of feeling hands raising them off the floor. The vibrations gave them the experience of levitating.

When I do a treatment, I ask the client to lie down on the floor on his or her back. I then surround the person with the seven bowls placed in alignment with each corresponding chakra, as follows:

- The A bowl at the throat chakra
- The B bowl at the crown chakra
- The C bowl at the sacral chakra
- The D bowl at the heart chakra
- The E bowl at the third eye chakra
- The F bowl between the legs (which is the root chakra)
- The G bowl at the solar plexus chakra

The treatment will balance one's chakras while helping to open them. Also, troubled areas in the body can experience healing or a shift in the pain level. I tell people that is the "airy-fairy" part of the therapy. The work is being done within, and we might not see the immediate results, but every single person I've worked with, even nonbelievers or people who have never meditated before, experience the journey and healing within. After about twenty minutes of playing the bowls, I am finished and will exit the room. People are usually in the room for an additional ten minutes, and some stay even longer. The transition back to the Beta state is a gentle return.

Once you have experienced the phenomenon of the Tibetan singing bowls, you know the true meaning of "surround sound."

CHAPTER TWENTY-FIVE

SURRENDER AND LETTING GO

You might have your own definitions of "surrender" and "letting go." In my experience, they are two different principles, with only a subtle difference between them. Both are important when speaking of our spiritual lives. Those who are conscious seekers, those people who have begun to awaken and know that true joy is only found in union with God or union with the present moment, have started the process of letting down their shields of resistance. Soon we realize that our distractions of people, places, and things no longer work; they no longer satisfy us. People who have stepped upon the spiritual path have one thing in common above all else: We are all called on to surrender and will continue to find ourselves letting go.

In the early years of my spiritual practice, I looked for the ultimate surrender, or the one that would bring me to the place of living in peace, able to move through life with ease. I soon realized that the final surrender was surrendering to the fact that I will always be surrendering. This attitude has enabled me to always return to the present moment, which invites a life of peace and living with ease.

Sometimes what leads us to surrender can be quite painful. Read and study the lives of any great mystics or saints, and you will see that they all went through great trials, often referred to as the "dark night of the soul." I have felt at times like I was being stripped of everything that I believed and felt I needed to maintain my identity. I let people know that I have walked through the fire on many occasions, and the field report is simple: The other side of surrender is pure loveliness.

Surrender is one of the most important principles for those making the commute to enlightenment. We must continue to adjust to the moment without trying to manipulate what life offers. Our vehicle on this journey is what, and who, is in front of us right now. We find our true identity when we surrender to The Now. This is enough. This is everything.

Unlike surrender, letting go doesn't mean giving up, but rather to move out of the way. Letting go can become a close companion as we move through the moments of our day, with our many plans and goals that can be interrupted in the twinkle of an eye. When we let go, we open our hearts to impermanence, and we find peace in the uncertainty that accompanies each moment. We discover that the spiritual path, although riddled with paradoxes and contradictions, is the path of least resistance. Over time we become cognizant that this new approach to life, by letting go and not trying to control outcomes, will actually empower us. All obstacles will begin to evaporate.

CHAPTER TWENTY-SIX

A MIND OF ITS OWN

When practicing meditation, we're immediately confronted with our minds. Our first response is to try to control our thoughts, and we soon realize that our minds actually have minds of their own. Probably one of the most frequently asked questions from a new student of meditation is "How do I shut off the thoughts?"

The answer is that there is no shortcut; we must keep watching each thought without attachment. Let them fly away as quickly as they appear. This simple truth can repel some seekers from continuing or beginning a meditation practice; others find comfort in this assurance and surrender fully.

Thoughts are like invisible warriors: Suddenly an army has invaded our minds. Left unattended, they turn into full-length scary movies, without a happy ending. In his masterpiece *Hamlet*, William Shakespeare noted that "When sorrows come, they come not single spies/But in battalions."

There is certainly a spiritual and meditation corollary to the Bard's words. Almost every story line has a true challenge at its beginning, a complete battalion of thoughts and desires, but through the experience of sitting through the drama we soon realize that the thoughts we create are complete fiction. When we finish our meditation, the curtain closes, the stage is dimmed, and we once again awaken to the truth that we can leave as an observer rather than a participant in the story that has just occurred in our minds.

Thoughts become feelings, and our feelings can be our barometer to signal to us that our thoughts are out of control. Through the continued practice of meditation, we see that we're not caught up in the challenge, but we're caught up in our negative thinking about it. Whatever life is presenting to us in this moment, it will become a worst-case scenario with our runaway thinking. This is why our practice is about returning to the moment and holding a space for what is really upon us. One negative thought will look for every opportunity to invite its friends to accompany it to the party. Practicing mindfulness is like watching a security camera. We can instantly see a negative thought when it tries to break in.

Practicing mindfulness lets us become aware that we are always thinking. This simple recognition is like asking each thought to show us its ID and passport. We don't deny these thoughts entry, but rather show them the exit door by skillful nonattachment. We learn to distinguish healthy thoughts from negative thoughts. Learning to live in the moment is like slowing down our minds. This won't eliminate the challenges that life throws at us, but those very same obstacles will never look as horrific when our thoughts are under observation.

Living life in the moment is having the right view of what is right in front of us. We learn to see that the obstacles we encounter are opportunities to deepen our spiritual practice. This practice enables your heart to be touched and then transformed by witnessing the birth of each new moment.

CHAPTER TWENTY-SEVEN

DESIRE AND LONGING

Our desire and longing to fill the emptiness within is what ultimately drives us to spiritual practice. Dark nights are followed by the rising sun. Our surrender to not knowing is how we begin to understand.

Some people spend a lifetime trying to fill the hole within, always looking to the outer world for completeness, to change their mood, or to be happy. Whatever they achieve or think they have gained seems to disappear as they try to hold on to what was chased after. Those who are fortunate eventually come to a place of great despair in their pursuit of that which is ultimately impermanent. The nightmare can become an enlightening realization, quite possibly a misunderstood gift and a blessing in disguise.

I speak from my heart and my own experience. I was once a hopeless addict whose life has been interrupted by a Higher Power. My life was transformed by surrendering to the principles of the Twelve Steps. Doing so has led to a life devoted to the practice of meditation and service to others.

Once our awakening begins, we turn our desire and longing within. Meditation is our vehicle, and we travel with it on the road to enlightenment. Desire and longing for union are essential. They are the fuel that keeps us coming back, keeps us meditating; however, attachment to the results will bring suffering in its wake.

We must be mindful not to hit the snooze button on the alarm and fall back asleep. Life by nature is unpredictable; it is a mystery and full of paradoxes. We have no way of knowing what we will be presented with in the next moment. The fear of the unknown will try to divert us to seek protection and to cling to what *seems real*, but the illusion somehow always slips from our grasp, no matter how hard we try to hold on. The spiritual path becomes the path that calls for surrender again and again; surrender turns our desperation into our search for divine union.

As seekers traveling on the spiritual path, we eventually admit that getting what we think we want or avoiding what we think is unpleasant are illusions that become a dance we no longer want to participate in. The obsession to acquire peace and fulfillment from any outside source is short-lived, and soon the same cycle starts up again. Our mantra is no longer "If I had more money" or "If I was married to my soul mate" or "If I lived in that house and drove that car, I would feel fulfilled."

Our meditation practice has led us to the present moment, where we embrace our new mantra, "If I can't be happy *now*, then *when*?" By being present, we pay close attention to what each moment offers. No matter how insignificant it might seem, a single instance can catapult us toward eternal joy.

Your desires and longings for oneness can awaken you each day with a wonderful anticipation of what each moment might bring. Each and every situation, pleasant or unpleasant, can be what ignites your transformation. The sudden gift of being present in the moment can feel like an awakening from amnesia.

The spiritual path will always call us to practice more meditation and to be of service to others. We continue to follow spiritual principles in our lives. Our transformation will begin to help others transform as well. Simply put, our responsibility is our ability to respond to the suffering we find around us. Let your desires and longings always be directed inward, and you will never sleepwalk through life again.

Think About This

I often meditate on the suffering that is all around me. At the same time, I believe that happiness, joy, and love are my true nature. The question that arises is, *Why there is so much suffering?* I don't know, but I do know there is so much loving kindness to give for those who want to serve others.

Cherish the life that is lived from within; it is called bliss.

When sitting to practice meditation as part of Step Eleven of the Twelve Steps, it becomes apparent to me that my mind has a mind of its own.

Observe your thoughts and let them go. This process works for me now and will in the near future.

Each new day contains a myriad of experiences and emotions. Some experiences have the potential to be traumatizing, while others can initiate a transformation. Traumatizing experiences can also be a gateway to transformation.

Do the footwork and know when to surrender; this is a groovy way to approach life.

Visions of walking through India and other holy lands may surface from deep within. It is likely that past life impressions or memories of a wandering monk or ascetic, during the soul's journey, will feel like you are being pulled by a magnet to the ongoing awakening from eons past. This desire to wander is replaced with a desire to practice meditation deeply. It is a journey toward the divine, which dwells within, and it is the true Holy Land.

The awakening of a spirit is the birth of a profound personality change. Then, as you move through life, people are profoundly touched by your presence; you become a channel for others to awaken. This is attraction rather than promotion. It is the way of twelve-step recovery programs and the practice of meditation.

While lying on the floor surrounded by seven singing bowls, each corresponding to a designated chakra, music from the bowls causes vibration to travel through the body, awakening the spiritual centers. The spirit moves like a lightning bolt deep within to levels of consciousness that might only be touched from days of continuous meditation.

Your passion for meditation is more important than the technique you choose to practice.

A simple thought can move my attention from the moment, obstructing the light of spirit, and I find myself standing in my own shadow.

Surrender, to me, is one of the sweetest of principles, something that I have to embrace daily. Surrender is part of every breath I take; to even think that I could conceive of what the next moment may hold is to cut myself off from an experience of pure love.

Meditation gently brings our minds back to the moment.

The simplicity of enlightenment is to be mindful of the present moment: This is enough; *this is everything.*

To follow your bliss, simply follow your breath.

The path of least resistance to samadhi is the next breath.

Grace is, to me, the times I feel I'm sitting in the lap of the divine.

When the mind drifts from the present moment, I forget my true nature. Suffering descends, and my view of my life and my being is darkened, much like the sun hiding behind a cloud.

Practicing mindfulness does not mean we will be free of challenges; what we will find is freedom in the midst of our challenges.

I want to be a mystic channeling love when I grow up.

Practice mindful listening today, and ordinary conversations might reveal the voices of angels.

Looking at life through your third eye of sight, you will see everyone engulfed in pure white light.

Great love and great suffering: either can streamline the path to bring the ego to a place of surrender, one of the first signposts you see on the spiritual path; *give . . . up . . . control.*

The sage understands and accepts that the path is riddled with contradictions and paradoxes as she walks with peace.

The practice of observing and not attaching to the thousand thoughts that come with each new dawn is essential, for they will incessantly overstate their importance.

Let go; be swept off your feet and fall into grace.

Paying attention, practicing meditation, and service to others can cause enlightenment to strike when you least expect it.

Showing up for meditation practice for forty-plus years has given me gifts. The message (gift) this morning was: *The act of lighting candles and incense is done with complete mindfulness.* I have been given permission to move to the next stage of sitting practice.

When we are living with great intention and attention, all movements become a spiritual practice.

By closing our eyes more often,
we will learn to see life with our hearts.

Working mindfully drowns out thoughts
of being somewhere else.

Paying attention to what is and serving others
are the true secrets to materializing happiness.

Need a new occupation? Become a miner.
Go within, and search for spiritual gems.

Where do the happiest people on the planet live?
In the present moment, wonderful moment.

Mindfulness turns all experiences into a prayer; I'm roused within for a deeper practice.

I don't have to know exactly what obstacle (opportunity) has been put in your path, but I can share three principles that I always turn to: surrender, equanimity, and impermanence; they change my view of life when I take the time to embrace their essence.

Consider the following:
Living in The Now is as simple as breathing.

Breathing = being alive.
Mindful breathing = being *blissfully* alive.

If you are seeking the immediacy of a spiritual connection, I suggest the simplicity of an exuberant devotion to this beautiful moment.

The challenge you observe arising within may be nonfiction, but the story you create about it is fiction.

Prepare for the next moment by being present for the one you are in.

Being fully present is the alarm that awakens the spirit.

Spiritual practice will rekindle your remembrance that *we are one*.

Since enlightenment is our true nature, our practice is to let go of what we're not.

Embrace renunciation today; give up dwelling on the past and worrying about the future.

The practice of meditation aligns us with the inner conditions that favor happiness.

When I'm not chasing and clinging to my desires, I'm giving up nothing but simplifying everything. I'm grateful each morning that I wake up and I'm breathing, but immediately the thoughts take hold and I know I have to follow that breath to truly "wake up."

CHAPTER TWENTY-EIGHT

SERVICE

Each morning I end my meditation practice with a prayer. I ask to have someone sent to interfere in my life. I was told early on by my first twelve-step sponsor and teacher that the barometer that indicates you're on the true path is when you awaken in the morning and your first thought isn't about self, but about how you can help someone else today.

People in twelve-step recovery are fortunate to have service as one of the fundamental aspects of their recovery to assure they won't return to active addiction. In order to have a daily reprieve from the obsession to use, it is highly suggested that we work with the newcomer. We must pass on what was freely given to us.

The cross-fertilization of meditation practice and selfless service is a paradigm that can give hope to the planet by changing the lives of all sentient beings. I believe that most spiritual movements are driven by the principle of service; be of service to others.

Once our awakenings start to happen, we may feel compelled to help others. This joy within that starts to arise *must* be channeled in service to others for it to continue. Enlightenment is a groovy experience, but it ends there if we don't start to give selflessly in every moment. The experience of awakening doesn't enlighten us, but the unconditional love we give away does.

In the Hindu religion there is a term called seva, which means service, or working for God. This reminds me of a story Ram Dass told. Ram Dass had the formal name of Richard Alpert. He was Timothy Leary's friend, and they became famous for their early experiments with LSD, but Richard ended up going to India and came back as Ram Dass. He and some other Westerners went to India seeking a guru. When they finally found the guru, he was on a hillside talking to a crowd of people. Someone asked Maharaji, meaning Great King, "How do we find enlightenment?" He smiled and said, "Serve people. Feed people." We can't get away from the fact that we have to give love, take no thought for self, and just be a channel of service.

In the Buddhist tradition, bodhichitta is the awakened heart of loving kindness and compassion. It is our natural state. In this consciousness, we see that we are part of every sentient being. When we have this knowledge of what really is, the spiritual journey is a commute we can't take by ourselves. We must make room for everyone to follow.

When bodhichitta is attained, we become a bodhisattva. We willingly take a vow to have as many rebirths as necessary in order to help all beings achieve enlightenment. In my first book, I talk at length about my first sponsor and teacher, Flobird. I would call her a bodhisattva. She devoted her life to helping others to find enlightenment.

When performing service, we must remember that it is called love and service, or loving action, putting love into action. The motivation for service is love. Without practicing the joy of serving, we begin to be motivated by ego; therefore, we must do our meditation practice each morning, step out, and look for places to practice acts of love.

Whatever a Higher Power or God may be, it seems to compel us to help others. The constant acknowledgment in the many faiths, religions, and mystical quests available is nearly always the same: Prayer and meditation combined with the practice of selfless service to others is imperative.

The great twentieth-century Hindu mystic Meher Baba offered us sound advice. He felt that no amount of meditation or prayer could do for us what helping others could do for us. Baba summarized both the recurring refrain and certain result of an ongoing spiritual practice: the inevitable goal of being of service to others. True enlightenment begins and ends with showing up for others in need.

CHAPTER TWENTY-NINE

PRAYER

I write and talk mainly about meditation, but in this chapter I want to explore prayer. A common analogy is that prayer is *talking* to God and meditation is *listening*. Being a member of twelve-step recovery and having worked the Twelve Steps many times over, I've been greatly influenced by the exact wording of Step Eleven: "We sought through prayer and meditation to improve our conscious contact with God as we understood Him, praying only for knowledge of His will for us and the power to carry that out."*

I want to focus on the part that says "praying only for knowledge of His will for us and the power to carry that out." How I interpret this statement is that it tells me not to pray for anything in my life or anyone else's, but to pray only for knowledge of God's will. To me this means that the highest form of prayer is done in silence—sitting, observing, and listening.

If we become so self-absorbed in asking for what we think we need or thinking about what others need to fulfill their life missions, then our busy minds are filled with thoughts of *wanting this* or *wanting that* and will never be able to receive guidance. Our imaginations shouldn't be focused on the existence of a heavenly

* Reprinted by permission of NA World Services, Inc. All rights reserved. The Twelve Steps of NA reprinted for adaptation by permission of AA World Services, Inc.

babysitter waiting to fill our every childish demand, but our egos will always try to negotiate and persuade us otherwise. Having a positive attitude about life and our ability to maneuver our way through its many obstacles is wonderful, but we need to be mindful of this magical thinking taking over. We could spend a lifetime of suffering as we wait for the manifestation of a divine being ready to fulfill our desires with the twinkle of the eye.

We are all caught in the cosmic dance of cause and effect, the law of karma. We must begin to understand that if we want the next moment to change, we must change our behavior in the present moment. Any of the spiritual practices we do each day will help us begin to be present and are important as we pave the way by moving ego and its relentless demands out of the way.

Life at times seems to be unfair, and we will feel compelled to pray for the healing of self or those close to us. When we find ourselves faced with such situations, our prayers for specific things can be followed by the words *Thy will be done*, or we can pray for the highest good to be done in our lives or in the lives of others. This type of practice will neutralize the prayer. It is our surrender to the moment, acknowledging our commitment to be present.

If we visit any church, temple, ashram, or group committed to spiritual practice, we can find prayers, chanting, and singing, praising whatever God the followers of the faith are embracing. Some use chanting and praying out loud as a way to give a more focused intention to their goal of contacting the divine.

In our time of deepest prayer, we will find it unnecessary to utter a prayer out loud. We come upon the realization that all is revealed in these times of spiritual yearning; love will know what we need in each moment. While sitting in silence, we simply listen; eventually we come face-to-face with our highest good. We need not manipulate what life offers us; we only need to embrace, accept, and surrender to the movement of the universe, to something greater than our false selves.

CHAPTER THIRTY

SILENCE

Mention the word *meditation*, and the image we most likely will conjure up is a tranquil setting. It could be a meditation room or hall, adorned with holy objects and painted in serene colors. Many prefer sitting in nature beside the ocean or a stream flowing down from the mountaintops. Numerous peaceful settings come to mind, but the common theme is always going to be silence.

Above all else, people crave silence while practicing meditation; most become agitated with any noise, which they feel distracts them from the moment.

I also enjoy a quiet setting. In 1991 my wife Bea and I bought a house on an acre of land on the Big Island of Hawaii. We moved there from Oahu in 1993, where we lived just feet away from our neighbors, easily hearing every toilet flush and every TV show they watched. After moving in, we snatched up the empty acres on each side of our property to encourage our solitude from noisy neighbors.

After a few years of this secluded living, we began to be invaded by tree frogs. I love the chirping of the birds surrounding our house. I can listen to them sing all day long, but the frogs start singing as the darkness descends and continue their choruses long after the birds go to bed. I happen to get up anywhere between 3:00 a.m. and 4:00 a.m. to sit for my morning meditation. *And now I'm joined by 10,000 frogs serenading me!* Although I do ask for the divine to put people in my life to disrupt things a bit, I thought, *10,000 frogs is a little over the top*. Yet I continue to share my morning meditation with them.

I prefer the outer silence, which would seem to make being in the moment and the transition to inner silence seem much easier, but meditation beckons us to be flexible and to embrace what the moment offers without trying to change it.

Most people who practice meditation aren't always sitting in a monastery high on a mountaintop. Many people have to practice in the middle of the city, with traffic and neighbors living life out loud. Whatever the conditions or setting you find yourself in, there will probably be distractions all around you.

The dog barking, the tree frogs singing, and the ambulance blaring its siren can all act as a mantra and bring you back to the moment. If outer noise reaches your awareness as you sit, be mindful if you are hearing this sound. If you are, then you are in the moment, because the sound is happening now, and it might just shock you out of a lengthy story line you are engaged in!

While we are sitting for meditation practice, we are taught to just observe all that arises and falls. We watch our thoughts and feelings come and go, appear and disappear, as quickly as they arrive. When sound begins to invade your senses, just sit and observe. You need not go to the sound, but rather just let it come to you. While we are observing all that is going on during our practice, we can step back and use our thoughts, feelings, and the noise that we hear to practice who is observing, and who is hearing the sound.

Without resistance and manipulation of what is, we soon can find ourselves going even deeper in the practice. This can be our introduction to true silence, the silence that is our true nature, the silence that lives deep within and cannot be disturbed by outer conditions. When we sit through whatever is rising and falling, we can suddenly find ourselves engulfed in what is commonly called "the sound of silence."

Many mornings the singing frogs move beyond distraction and seem to become my escort within. Unexpectedly, I find myself in the gap, the place between thoughts, a place of silence. The breath I was following is now undetectable, a place of emptiness that offers complete fullness. I'm content to sit and listen to the silence forever, but I become witness to the birth of my next thought, and the practice continues.

Yes, silence is golden, and most people would lean toward a place offering outer silence, but we know that even in a quiet place the chatter of the mind can soon become noisy, and even then meditation is cut short. Ultimately, meditation leads all of us to the place within where silence resonates. Even in the midst of chaos, we will look over our shoulders and find the peace of silence following in our footsteps. No matter what the conditions might be, we practice.

CHAPTER THIRTY-ONE

THERAPY AND STRESS REDUCTION

My relationship with mindfulness can be best described as a spiritual quest. I practice mindfulness because I consider that the doorway to enlightenment is found in the present moment. Mindfulness is not considered a religion, but it is practiced by members of many of the world's religions. Atheists and agnostics alike find mindfulness to be a technique they can practice with the same benefits as anyone who follows the traditions of a religion or other wisdom tradition. Because mindfulness is so versatile, it has found its way into all walks of life.

Most people will admit that their lives can be stressful at times. We all find ourselves faced with challenges such as illness of the body or struggles with emotional situations. We become lost in thoughts about the past or we think about what the future may hold. We are unable to remain in the present. By our living in the past and future, our lives can become one crisis after another. Soon we find ourselves buoyed by guilt from the past and anxieties about our future, and ultimately anchored in distress.

In the late 1970s, Jon Kabat-Zinn (previously referred to in Chapter Nine) brought the experience of meditation out of the ashrams and meditation halls and introduced the practice of mindfulness to the greater therapeutic community. It became obvious that meditation practice has profound medical and psychological benefits for those who practice this simple and gentle approach. The alleviation of chronic pain and severe mental distress has had such positive success that a myriad of wellness clinics and mind/body centers have adopted the mindfulness models.

Dialectical Behavior Therapy (DBT) was developed by Marsha Linehan, PhD, in 1993. DBT is the result of combining cognitive behavioral therapy with the practice of mindfulness. Psychologists are introducing the practice of mindfulness to their clients. It is a treatment modality based on teaching their clients to explore life as it occurs in the present moment and not to grasp at pleasant experiences or resist unpleasant ones. The idea is to pay close attention to life as it is happening, without judgment. Therefore, one would face the world, including its ups and downs, with more equanimity, encountering less stress and confusion, and in the process experience more joy and inner peace.

This technique works with even some of the most severe cases. DBT is also used to treat borderline personality disorder. The therapist works closely with the client, attempting to encourage and teach the client to become fully aware of his or her experiences in the present moment. In emphasizing the importance of experiencing thoughts and feelings—without criticizing oneself, any situation, or others who might be involved—DBT culminates in what is called radical acceptance. This proven technique teaches the client to tolerate situations without judgment or trying to manipulate the outcome.

Mindfulness has become the foundation of DBT skills, empowering the client to gain awareness of his or her feelings, thoughts, and behaviors. Awareness of life in the moment can help the client to avoid acting out in some severe way, causing self-harm or harming others. Neuroscience research using controlled studies shows that mindfulness makes positive and lasting changes to the brain. The Mindfulness Module enables the client to slow down and begin to be present; when anyone is present in his or her life, it becomes more difficult to act out with inappropriate behavior.

In an issue of *The Annals of Behavioral Science and Medical Education*, there is a report of a medical research study at Wake Forest Baptist Medical Center that estimates 20 to 60 percent of physicians will experience burnout at some time during their careers. This level of distress and strain can have a significant influence on the quality of care doctors provide patients. It can also decrease empathy and compassion for patients and increase the likelihood of medical errors. Accordingly, all third-year medical students at Wake Forest Baptist received guided relaxation and mindfulness meditation training known as Applied Relaxation and Applied Mindfulness (ARAM). The results, of course, have been favorable. Meditation works.

Why is mindfulness meditation working for people who have no inclination to grow spiritually from it? Why is it helping with chronic pain or severe depression? The answer to both questions is the simple ratio that I've talked about before: 10 percent of our suffering is caused by the actual events in our life, while 90 percent of our suffering is attributed to mental worry. Our reaction to life's challenges is more important than the actual challenges we face.

Many situations in life inevitably cause severe stress, intense emotional anguish, and even excruciating physical pain. If you're in a physical body on planet Earth, then stuff happens; life can seem to be relentless and even unforgiving at times. But if we stay present with what is arising, no matter what is happening, it will soften the experience: Remember, 10 percent of our stress and worry is from the actual situation; the other 90 percent is created solely from within our minds.

The continued practice of coming back to the present moment and not following the story line in our mind will eliminate the majority of the suffering we experience. Learn to give peace a chance by being in the moment. Be here now; this is the simplicity of mindfulness.

CHAPTER THIRTY-TWO

BRAIN FOOD

Twelve-step programs, along with other spiritual paths, have long suggested meditation as a means to improve one's "conscious contact" with God, higher power, or true nature, although scientific research stops short of proving that that's exactly what it does. There are many studies in medical and scientific journals that conclude that mindfulness meditation has the "godlike" ability to make positive changes to the physical structure of the human brain in as little as eight weeks.

In some cases, study participants were monitored to document the effects of mindfulness meditation on stress reduction. The studies demonstrate that changes in brain structure may underlie some of these reported improvements and that people are not just feeling better because they are spending more time relaxing. Magnetic resonance imaging (MRI) was taken of the brain structure of study participants two weeks before and then after they took part in the eight-week Mindfulness-Based Stress Reduction Program. Over a similar time interval, a set of MRI brain images were also taken of a control group of participants who didn't meditate.

Analysis of MRIs found increases in density of gray matter in the hippocampus, which is associated with memory and learning, and in brain structures known to be associated with self-awareness, introspection, and compassion. Participants in the study also reported a reduction in stress and were found to have decreased density of gray matter in the amygdala, known to play a role in regulation of stress and anxiety.

The practice of mindfulness meditation itself doesn't care why you meditate. Whether it's for a scientific research study, for stress reduction, or to recover from addiction as part of a twelve-step program, the results are the same.

In practicing mindfulness meditation, we learn to observe what is and accept what is going on, finding ourselves embracing equanimity, a principle that most likely eluded us during our active addiction. Mindfulness keeps us in the moment—The Now. We come to see that our stress arises mainly from thinking of what *might* happen tomorrow, next week, or even within the hour. These stories we produce in our minds are always worse than any actual outcome; however, the practice of mindfulness keeps inviting us back to the moment we are in, where all is well.

Scientific research is now proving what practitioners have known for centuries: Meditation works. Perhaps the changes to the physical structure of the brain that researchers are now verifying are parallel to the psychic changes necessary for continuing growth and connectedness provided by a daily spiritual practice.

CHAPTER THIRTY-THREE

RIGHT NOW

The simplicity of life is that there is only now. Suffering happens when we are caught in the undertow of our thoughts and are pulled away from the present moment. In meditation practice, we learn to constantly observe until we become a calm *observer* of our thoughts, rather than a panicking participant. When we drift from the moment, we gently return, again and again. We always start over right now, right where we are.

We think that we will begin living in The Now once we get our lives together: maybe tomorrow or next week. Soon it becomes next year, and we are still trying to organize our lives into some imagined ideal of order or success. We have to start now; if not, then when? No matter how despondent we may feel about what situation we're in, it's the perfect time to embrace what is. Sometimes the more hopeless we feel, the more it will encourage our hearts to crack wide open, and we will stumble into the moment.

Our commitment to continue our practice will soon surprise us with important insights: that true enjoyment comes from living in the moment, and that our story lines, our own thinking, are what keep us from the precious moment. We begin to see that we don't have to worry unnecessarily and manipulate our lives to assure our future. The best preparation is to live our lives fully in this present moment. Bliss cannot be coerced. But it can be invited in through the doorway of meditation. This is what we have been striving for all along, but when living at warp speed, we have completely missed bliss. The simple answer is this: We must slow down to experience every moment.

The story of the woman, the tigers, and the strawberry is a perfect example of living in the present moment. A woman is walking through the jungle when suddenly she is confronted by a tiger, and she begins to run away. The tiger is gaining on her. She comes to the edge of a cliff. She climbs over the edge and hangs on to a vine. When she looks down, she sees more tigers excitedly looking up at her. At the same time, she notices a mouse chewing away at the vine she is clinging to. She also sees a beautiful red strawberry growing within arm's reach. She looks up, looks down, looks at the mouse, and then reaches to pick the strawberry. She then pops it in her mouth, enjoying it thoroughly. Our lesson is to reach for the strawberry in every moment, no matter how despairing our situation may seem.

As we move through life, we will always have a tiger above and a tiger below; challenges come and go. Through our continued practice, we will learn to look for the loveliness that every moment has to offer.

CHAPTER THIRTY-FOUR

BECOMING VULNERABLE

Meditation wears away at our egos like a river flowing over rocks; after thousands of years the river smoothes the sharp edges and polishes the rocks to their natural beauty. As our egos become worn away, our true nature is revealed, which above all else is vulnerable, compassionate, and kind. The Hindu mystic Ramana Maharshi described this experience. Happiness is your nature; it's not wrong to desire it. What is wrong is seeking happiness outside when it is inside.

The further we travel down the spiritual path, the more we begin to shed what we are not. As our false self peels away, the ego begins to lose its grip and the suggestive power it seems to have over our lives. When this precious vulnerability emerges, we have no choice but to gradually continue to let go of old ideas of who and what we thought we were. Instead, we invite and welcome new beliefs of who we really are. We become teachable when the ego is deflated.

The theme of our meditation practice has always been about returning to the moment. When finding ourselves hijacked by our thoughts, we return to our breath and start over again and again. This practice of starting over again and again is what gives us strength when facing challenges. We learn to get up right where we fall down. This is yet another paradox of spirituality that goes against the highly Western idea of "standing your ground": The more open we become to being vulnerable, the more letting go and surrender become part of our lives. Anyone consciously traveling on the spiritual path usually has this characteristic of letting go and surrender in the forefront of their lives.

Being stripped of our old ideas may seem painful, but in hindsight we begin to see it as a gift. When we stand naked in the present moment, clothed no more by our false ideas of security and our constant drive to cling to anything on the outside for a moment of relief, this is the birth of true freedom and peace. This is the awakening of spirit.

The wonderful moment, present moment is where we meet face-to-face with our true nature. After this introduction, it becomes essential for our continued awakening that we live and manifest that which we begin to glimpse in our deepest insights. When we change our thinking, our actions seem to change accordingly.

When we move through life in The Now, we walk holding hands with the imperfection of our human nature and the perfection of our divine nature. Resolve now to touch the joy of your true nature while becoming friendly and accepting of what arises each moment from your human nature.

To the extent that we are sincere in knowing ourselves, we help heal the world. We must become willing to go through the initiations of being present, embracing the love and joy of The Now, and at the same time become willing to feel the suffering of the world, standing unprotected, living only to serve others.

In the end, it's about The Now and being totally present with the darkness or the light, with anything the moment offers—nothing to hang on to, nowhere to hide, standing naked in The Now.

We have to give up everything (ego) and expect nothing in return. Becoming vulnerable means allowing things to be *as they are*. Practice, practice, practice, and have a rendezvous with God (true nature).

CHAPTER THIRTY-FIVE

GRATITUDE

"If the only prayer you ever say in your entire life is thank you, it will be enough."

—Christian mystic Meister Eckhart

My first spiritual teacher and twelve-step sponsor, Flobird, introduced me to the Twelve Steps of recovery and was the main influence in my beginning journey down the spiritual path, and always spoke of having an "attitude of gratitude." She explained how gratitude and humility walk hand in hand. Humility brings us to a place where we know, no matter what, that we are not the doer; we are simply channels. This process gets ego out of the way and opens the door wide for gratitude to flourish, and influences our attitude with whatever life presents us. Flobird's teachings can be found in my first book, *The Mindful Addict*.

We learn to accept praise and rejection with the same attitude of gratitude, for we have arrived at a very special place where we don't have to be right or we don't have to be in control, we merely need to be thankful and embrace our role as a channel to serve others. When living in the moment, we don't need to project to the future and think, *If this or that happens, I will be happier*.

We reach for gratitude right here in this moment and give thanks. When being present, we surrender to what is. By not wishing or manipulating change, we accept what the moment offers and our gratitude arises naturally.

Stop each day to be with the breath, and either write a gratitude list or just count your blessings in that moment. No matter what life throws at us, we can find something to be grateful for.

People who embrace gratitude are able to see loveliness or the hand of the divine in everything. Gratitude is our path to learning from everyone we meet and every situation; it keeps us grounded, willingly humble, and teachable.

Not all people are easy to be around, not all situations in life are easy to endure, but gratitude will always keep our hearts open to learn from each experience and everyone who somehow touches or affects our lives.

Gratitude, like any spiritual principle, requires training the mind. But as with meditation, we just keep starting over again and again. Soon we glimpse the magic of each moment and suddenly realize we have always been on the path and that all of life is holy.

CHAPTER THIRTY-SIX

JUST WORK IT

In twelve-step meetings, it is common to hear the phrase "working the steps." You also hear people talk about "living the steps." Both statements are true. To live the steps, I believe you have to work them first, and in the order that they are written, in conjunction with the guidance and experience of a sponsor. A general rule of thumb is that there is only one "wrong" way to work the steps: alonc and by yourself.

Even after forty-plus years, I *still* work the steps. This means that I touch on what each step is saying to me at this stage of my recovery. I write out the steps. The work involves self-discovery and digging deep into what my life and the twelve-step process are saying to me in this moment.

I want to focus on Step Eleven of the program, which refers to meditation and prayer: "We sought through prayer and meditation to improve our conscious contact with God as we understood Him, praying only for knowledge of His will for us and the power to carry that out." Prayer and meditation require a lot of diligent work and discipline. This could easily turn out to be some of the hardest work we do in our lives, and I see no retirement plan in the future.

I love the work. I equate the practice of meditation with having job security for the rest of my life.

There are meditation teachers, but no one can do this for us. We may read countless books on meditation, follow the teachings of a veritable school of gurus, and attend dozens of retreats, yet we must personally experience the difference between an intellectual understanding of these concepts and the actual reality of a spiritual practice.

Only we can do the work it takes to show up, familiarize ourselves with the constant rising and falling of our thoughts, and let what we are not fall away. The paradox is that as we awaken, we see that we have always been what we seem to attain. We also see that we really have no power to make it happen. Meditation is a return to the present moment; we begin to understand that we are also returning to who we are.

I know this to be true; each awakening has come as a gift, and I've done nothing—so why keep showing up?

The spiritual journey is one that is directed by one paradox after another. Paradox is the compass and meditation is the vessel. Once we begin to meditate, we find ourselves compelled to keep showing up; the process itself becomes fulfilling.

The saying goes that "you must lighten up to first experience enlightenment." Meditation to me is serious, yet I'm told not to be so serious. I have realized that by my showing up each day, it has almost become effortless, a kind of choiceless decision. I arise each morning to sit and truly be in the process of waking up.

As the false self begins falling away, we are pulled into our own calling to stay present and realize what in Vedic teachings is called the Atman, or true self.

A life spent paying attention to each moment takes incredible practice, patience, and work. An awakening implies that we have been unawake, unlike being asleep and just drifting through life and being misdirected by distractions, and never being truly present. Instead, we have been living in the past or future and blaming life's events for feelings that arise and fall away. Once we start to wake up to the present moment, wonderful moment, we need never turn back. Having a glimpse at life through mindfulness, we resolve to do whatever it takes to be present with each breath.

Our daily practice can be enhanced by attending retreats. Retreats are not a vacation featuring incense. They are designed and implemented to deepen our practice. Meditating under the guidance of a teacher with a group of people can be highly beneficial and educational. Yet we must apply what we have learned in our daily lives.

We hold day-long retreats at our house several times a year. These retreats consist of sitting meditation, walking meditation, and dharma talks, all usually held between 9:00 a.m. and 4:30 p.m. At the end of the day, I'm more worn out than if I had worked a grueling day of manual labor. Yet the benefits of practicing far outweigh the hard work experienced at a retreat. We keep showing up; we keep working it; we just do it.

Insights to Ponder

True joy waits outside the gates of our self-centered prison; the key is to serve others.

Lasting joy is not found in a collection of things. The principle of impermanence assures us that we will be visited by suffering; a favored choice of the sage is to live life mindfully, practicing the wonderful moment, beautiful moment.

With the realization that we can't sidestep our karma, we promptly learn to embrace surrender and acceptance.

The veil of Maya is so thin that the breeze from one breath can let us through; simply be mindful when you breathe.

Meditation is the practice of observing and not attaching to my *internal affairs* as they arise. This daily practice soon finds its way to my *external affairs.* Observing and not attaching can cause peace and joy in the midst of daily challenges.

HELP WANTED: Apply within.

Don't let anxiety be your new drug of choice.
To get clean, just return to the moment.

Practice until your hair stands on end; practice
until the serpent at the base of your spine awakens.
As it rises and touches each chakra, it will be like
10,000 volts exploding. Now you will only find
fulfillment in serving others.

Our commute on the spiritual path and our
practice of living in the moment does not equal
a life of passive existence; rather, it calls forth
a life of active participation.

Being unable to accept life's offering in this moment,
I'm refusing the fullness of my existence.

Sitting, observing, embracing,
I'm speechless, lost in the love.

The practice of equanimity is a shortcut to acceptance,
lightening the workload of surrender.

To realize my true nature, I must cease being what I
thought I wanted to be, and just breathe with attention.

The spiritual journey is one you can't travel by yourself; you must bring everyone with you.

Going on retreat is not to separate ourselves from others, but to learn to embrace all of life with compassion.

The path calls for us to follow a light that most don't see, and at times our own shadow blinds us; we just take the next step.

My joy is greater when I share it with you.

If you want to simplify your life by renunciation, then give up resentment and judgment.

Living in the past or the future can be detrimental to your mental health.

The present moment is ubiquitous, yet most wander in moments of another time; continue to practice the presence.

Willingness to sit with what arises, again and again, will evoke a passage to our true nature, where peace can be found in the most horrific challenges.

When you taste the true joy of practice, living life with mindfulness becomes a primary goal.

The spiritual principle of impermanence is spelled out in the popular twelve-step slogan "This too shall pass." Even the "dark night of the soul" will vanish with the rising sun; serving others will hasten the light.

Sitting with what arises, I'm convinced there is no better alternative.

Living the dharma fulfills your karma and eliminates the drama; please serve others.

All I am saying is give peace a chance; gently return to the breath.

Addiction was my initiation to begin the awakening within. This insidious disease is often misunderstood; for many, it becomes the vehicle to a life of grace.

With each surrender, ego will make a mad dash at something else to hang on to for identity; the conclusion is to surrender to the fact that we will always be surrendering.

Hear the sound of an ancient gong echoing off the mountains. Smell the scent of flowers as it blows through the temple. Sit and watch your breath, again and again.

Each challenge is an opportunity to dive deeper within.

Observe your thoughts, but listen to your heart;
that's where God dwells.

Live beautifully in the world,
while practicing mindfulness.

Awaiting my next assignment. . . . Okay, I got it.
Serve others.

If you're feeling bored or lacking direction in your life, then take a moment, be with your breath, and ask to be guided to serve another; it's simply magic.

Nothing is ordinary in the present moment.

Meditating with eyes closed enables us to see
life more clearly with our heart.

Dwelling on self has never worked, yet it's
fascinating how easy it is to do.

The practice of mindfulness will keep us adjusting
to what life offers and demands of us.

CHAPTER THIRTY-SEVEN

BEGINNER'S MIND

If I filled out a spiritual résumé, it would read something like this:

- I became a vegetarian in 1966.
- I began meditating that same year.
- I attended my first twelve-step meeting in 1968.
- I have been clean since October 20, 1971.

I'm certainly not a beginner at meditation practice and am called an oldtimer in the recovery arena; but in both cases I like to keep what is called a beginner's mind. I feel safest when I'm feeling vulnerable because I remain teachable.

Suzuki Roshi, the Japanese Zen Master who founded the San Francisco Zen Center, spoke of how in a beginner's mind many possibilities existed, but that in an expert's mind there were few.

I ceased being a newcomer in recovery and at meditation years ago. I've been consistent with both practices for over forty years. The accumulation of these years has not made me an expert in either realm, but that very same ceaseless desire to show up has graced me with discipline. I still participate in my recovery, and although I have missed occasional days of meditation in the past,

I honestly cannot remember a time in the last several years when I didn't show up for practice first thing in the morning.

Having a beginner's mind-set in meditation becomes quite easy as you continue your practice. You eventually realize that on many occasions you will sit down to meditate and spend that entire duration drifting aimlessly within your mind. When people consider approaching a meditation technique, they invariably balk: "But I can't quiet the mind." The irony and paradox of this response is the truth that this is the entire practice. Our ego doesn't go on vacation when we sit in meditation. The practice occurs when we return to our method of choice (breath, mantra, etc.) and navigate through this eternal rising and falling of our thoughts, feelings, and emotions. Sometimes ten or fifteen minutes can easily pass, and suddenly you remember what you're doing.

In these instances, you certainly don't feel like a so-called expert. But to sit and embrace these inevitable realities of meditation can be the very things that drive us back to the meditation cushion every time. Once we visit the moment, we quickly experience that The Now is all there is, and it is always new, refreshed, and reloaded by the impermanent nature of reality. We experience the freshness and wonderment from being present and see that the beginner's mind is available constantly; every moment is an adventure, every moment offers us a surprise, and every new moment becomes our current teacher.

By staying active in my recovery, I receive the same gift. I don't feel like a newcomer in the sense that I'm frightened I will use again, but I feel reverence and awe for my life. Each time I go through the steps, I have a feeling of being unrestricted in the spiritual growth that might happen in the process.

I try to live my life to the fullest each moment, but to do this I must renew my commitment and find strength to face the many challenges that will appear. I do this by showing up for my spiritual practice. I don't depend on some theory that I might read in a book or rely merely on a maxim voiced by a guru, however profound or even true it may be. It has been said that the spiritual life is not a theory; it must be lived. Living it means practicing it in each moment, sometimes falling short, but getting up from where we are and continuing onward without doubt or regret. We just need to keep an open mind and increase our desire to know ourselves. An open mind is a beginner's mind.

CHAPTER THIRTY-EIGHT

SIMPLICITY

The spiritual path invites us to give up living with the idea that life is always going to be stressful. We find we can simplify things, begin to live in the moment, and awaken to things as they are. *Sounds simple enough.* The truth is it is simple, but without discipline this new life soon becomes out of reach to us all.

Discipline comes from the word *disciple.* A disciple is someone who is willing to learn from another. In his writings, Paramahansa Yogananda said that if one would sit in meditation for twenty-four hours, with his mind completely focused on God and self-realization, he would attain enlightenment. The Buddha encouraged his monks by stating that those who practiced diligently would be enlightened in seven days; and if not in seven days, then seven months or seven years. The key that unlocks these promises is discipline. Anyone on the spiritual path would be happy even with the "seven-year" promise, but for most the awakenings will come at a slower pace.

Many who have read these promises have put them to the test; I know I have. But in my daily practice, I'm lucky to go ten minutes before finding myself wandering somewhere in the deep recesses of my mind, as if I had developed amnesia and totally forgot my goal of holding hands with the present moment as it unfolds to the next.

The practice of mindfulness is quite simple. To begin, we just try to follow our breath; we find a pleasant setting outside or create a space in our house. We have to do nothing else, no years of study to pass a test that says you can now be conscious of what you have always been doing: breathing. Yet this simple and pleasant act takes discipline to show up for each day. We never want to condemn ourselves for missing days; we just keep trying to show up. If we miss, we try again tomorrow. Our willingness to show up turns into discipline, and I think what is sometimes referred to as "grace" enters. We then find that our daily meditation is as important as our daily intake of food.

When we are disciplined, we become disciples of each moment; our hearts open to learn from each experience, challenges become less stressful, and we begin to see them as a way to dive deeper within. We notice that each moment can offer genuine happiness, just because we are sitting still, free from any ego-driven agenda. Abruptly, and to our surprise, the stress falls away, life and practice become the same, and we recognize the simplicity of each moment.

CHAPTER THIRTY-NINE

NOTHING BUT LOVE

As the spirit continues to awaken, the heart continues to open. This awakening and opening are the purpose of the spiritual path and our life's work. As we venture into this new life, even with our first few steps, we begin to sense that in the end it's going to be about love. It seems to be the main principle of existing in the moment. Love is the adhesive that holds the universe together.

Most spiritual teachings, like twelve-step recovery, will have steps to take, telling us which steps to take first, second, third, and so forth, so as not to confuse the student about what should come before and what should come after. The end result is always about learning to give unconditional love, meaning we begin to move the focus from ourselves to others. While being in service to others, we are sidestepping our ego, and we begin to move closer to thinking of others and their needs instead of ours.

I spent my first ten years of consciously walking this path with the lady that introduced me to the Twelve Steps. Flobird was my teacher and sponsor, and by her daily actions she taught me about giving love and asking for and expecting nothing in return. I found out firsthand and early on that unconditional love is our essence.

Our lessons are simple but necessary: In the beginning of recovery, we learn to reach out to someone newer to the Twelve Steps than ourselves. The act of giving someone a ride to a meeting might be our first experience of doing something without an agenda or to receive something back. Flobird referred to this practice as "love without a price tag."

I believe Charlotte Joko Beck, an American Zen teacher, taught that enlightenment is the ability to give completely in every second. It isn't about some great experience.

What does it mean to give in the moment? For example, when the phone rings, how can we give? When doing physical work—cleaning, painting, cooking—what does it mean to give totally? So please give, give, give, and practice, practice, practice. It is the way.

In my early years of "on-the-job training"—while learning the gift of love and thinking of others—I had to learn not to put people in boxes or categories. I saw how attractiveness played a big part in this type of thinking. If someone was considered hip, slick, and cool by me, then it was easy to embrace them and let them into my life. This attitude undercut so many people, and restricted any love and compassion I might have had, merely because of some outer illusion and impermanent or even misleading situation or encounter. When practiced, I found equanimity to be a principle that started to include many more people in my life. This constant labeling and compartmentalizing of people and situations is what separates all of us from love.

The Buddha taught that we are never separated from enlightenment. Even at those times when we feel most stuck, we are never alienated from the awakened state. We all carry the Buddha nature, or the Christ nature; it is who we are. We can refer to both of these natures as our true nature or love nature. How can we be separated from what we really are?

What Flobird taught is what all spiritual teachers emphasize and live each day: an extraordinary and selfless love. By following the steps of any spiritual path, we find ourselves starting to live by spiritual principles, which in themselves will start the awakening of spirit and the opening of the heart. This occurs sometimes slowly, even over the course of a lifetime, and at other times these epiphanies can be explosive as our true nature ignites upward to the top from deep within. We come to a place where no matter what we feel like, we find ways to put love into action. Soon we have no choice. It has become our path home, and we are pulled like a magnet within. What we find within must be shared with others. True love has to keep giving.

CHAPTER FORTY

FOLLOW YOUR BLISS

The philosophy of Joseph Campbell is often summarized by the phrase "Follow your bliss." Campbell began sharing this idea with students during his lectures in the 1970s. Although this is one of his most quoted phrases, he felt it was the most misunderstood.

Some might interpret bliss as having the perfect life: marriage, money, and all our dreams fulfilled. The most common example is the right career: doing what you *want* to do. The trouble with having a fantasy of the ideal is that things are constantly changing.

We all live with the law of impermanence, so when things change, what happens to our bliss? This was the misunderstanding that people had with "Follow your bliss." They understood it to be hedonism, or a life of pleasure.

Following your bliss is like following one moment into the next; our bliss is here now. Our dreams should be flexible possibilities, not rigid desires. If you follow your bliss, then you see yourself on a path that has been there all the while, waiting for you; the life that you *ought* to be living turns out to be the one you *are* living. Wherever you are, if you are following your bliss, you are enjoying that life within you, all the time.

Our bliss has nothing to do with us trying to create the circumstances we think we need in order to be happy. It is living a life of mindfulness, always able to applaud and be thankful for what each moment offers us.

I'm a huge fan of positive thinking. We're always thinking, so why not have it be positive, supportive, and encouraging to our awakening? But I'm not an advocate of trying to create what I think I need. I know about the "God Box," I am aware of *The Secret,* and I'm sure they both work. But who among us is really reaping those benefits from merely writing down our dreams or thinking our way into paradise? We know desire is okay, but our attachment is the adhesive element to any dream that causes the heartache.

I take a firm stand in reality. I have no idea what I need in my life to be happy. I have no idea what I need that might awaken me. I choose to sit and embrace what is in my life, give thanks for whatever it teaches me, and move gently with the flow to the next moment and do it all over again. With each inhalation and exhalation, I will be following my breath. I will be following my bliss.

CHAPTER FORTY-ONE

SYNCHRONICITY

The continued practice of meditation may cause the phenomenon of synchronicity to occur more often—or does it make us more aware of something that has always been happening? What is synchronicity? The dictionary defines it as such: "the coincidental occurrence of events and especially psychic events (as similar thoughts in widely separated persons or a mental image of an unexpected event before it happens) that seem related but are not explained by conventional mechanisms of causality."* These coincidences were explored heavily in the psychology and writings of Carl Gustav Jung.

This phrase found its way into society in the 1960s, but Jung introduced the concept as early as the 1920s. It wasn't until 1951 that Jung first offered a full statement of his views, and the following year he published a paper on the phenomenon. Jung was transfixed by the idea that life was not a series of random events but rather an expression of a deeper order. Jung believed that synchronicity was an ever-present reality for those who have eyes to see it. I love this idea, for it correlates with my understanding of God. In recovery,

* By permission. From *Merriam-Webster's Collegiate® Dictionary* ©2014 by Merriam-Webster, Inc. (www.Merriam-Webster.com).

we talk about God as we understand God. I've said for several years now that, after forty-plus years in my recovery program, I have no understanding of God. What I do see is that the universe is *for me* and not *against me*. Something extraordinary is happening; it is not random, and I want to serve it.

The ideas of Jung and Einstein as well, with whom Jung communicated at length about this extraordinary phenomenon, can be found in the papers Jung presented in 1952. As we start to awaken and practice meditation, we are more likely to start experiencing "happy accidents."

Early in my recovery, I was introduced to the idea that if I put this very life into service, carrying the message to the newcomer first and foremost, I no longer would have to be constantly ruled by the self-centered thinking of my own life. I would always find myself in the right place at the right time, and all my needs in the moment would be cared for.

I spent my first ten years of recovery traveling with my teacher Flobird, who carried the message to me in 1968. I experienced many times over the miracle of synchronicity. The teachings were simple: Show up for meditation each day, listen for guidance, and dare to act on it by stepping into the unknown, with the ultimate motivation being to serve others. This lifestyle we led encouraged what I called modern-day miracles, finding ourselves in the right place at the right moment, and synchronicity occurring again and again.

I have called those earliest years of recovery "on-the-job training." In many ways it was easy. I was mesmerized by this new life, and followed the guidance of Flobird while I was learning to trust in my own growing and intuitive sense of right and wrong. I was shown over and over again that I was provided for in each moment. Synchronicity had become yet another loving teacher discovered through my surrender to the practice of meditation.

In my personal life, I've had so many coincidences accumulate that I cannot label them as random occurrences or dice rolls of the universe. Synchronicity may not be able to be explained in a science lab, nor can it be understood by our minds, but if we understand grace or karma, then we can understand that the two seem to be related. Both may only be truly understood in the deep and infinite silence within each one of us.

I have shown many examples of synchronicity in my first book, *The Mindful Addict*. Here is one example taken from its pages: "Onc of my favorite moments of guidance occurred when my wife and I were leaving for India in the mid-1990s. We made our reservations to go, but we didn't pay for the ticket until right before leaving. Yet our seats were held for us."

About eight or nine days before we were supposed to depart, my business was in debt, so there was doubt regarding whether this was even the right, let alone responsible, thing to do. I went into the meditation room and closed the door. I sat in silence, asking for a clear message as to whether we were going to India or not. The money situation was not good, but I knew deep within my heart that I was willing to make this journey and carry the message of recovery.

There was a recovery convention in Kolkata, and the organizers wanted me to come speak. Knowing my motive was in the right direction, always coming back to service, I sat there in silence, but nothing was coming through. After a while, I blew out the candles and left the meditation room. As I walked out and closed the door, the phone rang. I answered it. It was someone from the Wood Valley Buddhist Temple, which is located in Pahala, about an hour's drive from our house. Eight months prior, they had had a fundraiser where we had donated $100. They had just held the drawing, and we had just won first prize—a round-trip ticket to India. There was our answer: We were going to India.

I'm sure Jung or Einstein would have loved the above example of synchronicity in its purest and most beneficial form. I always encourage people to practice being present and to be awed by each new moment and the gifts that will be revealed if we merely pay attention.

CHAPTER FORTY-TWO

LIVING THE DHARMA

Words carry vibrations, and the word *dharma* resonates within when I read the word or even hear it mentioned. Many people have been introduced to the dharma, a Sanskrit word, by the influx of Buddhism in the West. The popular meaning to most people has become "the teachings of the Buddha," but also in Buddhism it means "cosmic order." In some respects, the Buddha was essentially a reformer of Hinduism, the faith where the concept of dharma originated. In Hinduism, the oldest surviving religion, dharma means "living within the natural order."

Personally, when I refer to the dharma it is associated with the teachings of the Buddha and the principles of the Twelve Steps. This is because dharma, in the broadest sense, means "spiritual teachings."

Religious scholars have written volumes about the teachings of the Buddha. The Buddha's first and simplest teaching was the Four Noble Truths or the Eightfold Path, which I referred to in a previous chapter. The simple message of the dharma from the Buddha has to do with letting go of our story line and embracing what is. In other words, what is happening right now in your life is a vehicle for waking up. This uncomplicated message is a refrain throughout this book.

The simplicity of the twelve-step programs and the Four Noble Truths is that once you start to apply either to your life, you might notice and enjoy as your older ideas, views, and behaviors begin dropping away, to be replaced by new ideas and actions. I've seen miracles occur in the realm of recovery, when someone who, only a month previously, might have been passed out in the gutter due to using suddenly wakes up with a sparkle in his or her eyes. Some experiences aren't so immediate and take more time. But a step in the right direction in this moment will make a future moment that much more wonderful.

In his teachings, the Buddha repeatedly encouraged his followers to not just believe his words, but to experience this "waking up" by practicing each day. We are not asked to sit in a class and study spiritual teachings; we are guided by our spiritual teachers or sponsors to live the dharma or the Twelve Steps. When we put these teachings into action on a daily basis, our meditation will begin to calm and awaken our hearts and minds. Meditation has the power to change both our thinking and our behaviors. We will begin to experience the birth of living one moment at a time. The spiritual path isn't some theory or ideal, but rather a practice that empowers us to live in each moment, step away from the struggles that life seems to place in front of us, and see things as they really are.

The heart of the dharma is simple: Stop clinging to what we see as pleasurable and resisting what seems uncomfortable, and always return to the breath, resting with what the moment offers. Grasp at nothing. Resist nothing. Let it be.

Living the dharma means we practice throughout the day, not just in our morning prayers and meditation, but in every moment. The acclaimed beat poet and visionary Allen Ginsberg was a practicing Buddhist who studied and practiced Eastern religious disciplines extensively. Ginsberg used the expression "surprised mind." You sit down and wham! A nasty surprise arises. So be it. We don't reject it but compassionately acknowledge and then note this occurrence as "thinking" and let it go. Then . . . wow! A delicious surprise appears. This surprise is not to be clung to but is instead lovingly recognized as "thinking," and we simply let the thought go.

My thoughts always bring me back to equanimity. They will continue to rise and fall, and any power I bestow upon them will only be the beginning of yet another story line.

Milarepa, a Tibetan yogi and saint, taught that the mind has more projections than there are dust particles in a sunbeam, and that even hundreds of spears couldn't put an end to this phenomenon. We continue our practice of observing these inevitable mental visitors and try not to attach to them. When we embrace, acknowledge, and ultimately let go of these thoughts, we see them for what they truly are: just the ego engaging in its nonstop job of thinking.

CHAPTER FORTY-THREE

THE SOUND OF MUSIC

Music has played an intricate part in meditation or spiritual ceremonies for centuries. It can be found in some form or another even in the most primitive tribes, used to inspire deep meditation and even trancelike states. The sound is used to transport one to transcendental states.

Music is a two-way conversation, ultimately a never-ending communication and dialogue between sentient beings: the performer, the listener, and, in spiritual chanting or singing, the listener-turned-participant. Where does the inspiration begin and end? Someone is inspired to write the notes and lyrics of every song, and these musical notes then inspire the listener with joy or some creative endeavor. If the music dies, does inspiration die as well?

Visit any church, and music is invariably part of the service. People are singing about God or to God. We all have been touched by the Southern Baptist singers; the whole congregation is on their feet dancing. Visit iTunes or Pandora Internet Radio and type "meditation music" into the search field and the choices are endless, ranging from New Age to Indian classical music.

Collective group chanting accompanied by the playing of instruments such as the sitar, harmonium, and tabla drums in India is called *kirtan.* Paramahansa Yogananda was an early proponent of kirtan singing in the West, chanting Guru Nanak Dev's "Hay Hari Sundara" ("Oh God Beautiful") with 3,000 people at Carnegie Hall in 1923.

Since that time, a wave of kirtans has found its way to the West. In the late sixties, composer and sitar virtuoso Ravi Shankar teamed up with George Harrison following The Beatles' 1968 initiation into Transcendental Meditation under the tutelage of Maharishi Mahesh Yogi. This then-unusual summit helped bring kirtans into the limelight with songs like Harrison's 1970 number-one single "My Sweet Lord," which introduced the Hare Krishna chant to popular music. Today, Krishna Das is one of the key proponents, devotees, and performers of kirtans, touring regularly around the world and keeping this direct blending of spirit and music in the hearts and minds of many. People are chanting across the nation. The teachings of the Buddha have brought with them the captivating sound of Tibetan monks chanting.

Their deep, guttural, vocal sound is quite hypnotic, and while listening to their sacred chanting it can feel as if one is lifted up beyond worldly cares. The monks and devotees use the music of chanting to recite various sacred texts.

While recovering from prostate surgery in 1999, I played tapes of Buddhist monks chanting every day. I considered the time spent listening as a direct and positive influence on both my recovery and my healing from the medical procedure.

Occasionally a simple musical note can ignite our awakening. It need not be what we formally call meditation music, church music, or even chanting. For me personally, listening to a Van Morrison song can arouse an awakening within me. Morrison's music and similar genres were on the soundtrack that I played while writing my first book, *The Mindful Addict*.

Ultimately, any musical genre, whether it is pop, rock, classical music, or chanting, works if it touches your heart and affects your true self. When our hearts are open, our spirits are in an awakened state. These conditions can catapult us back to the moment, and that's enough; that's everything.

CHAPTER FORTY-FOUR

MINDFUL EATING

Like breathing and walking, eating is something we do every day, and most of the time we are unaware, if even conscious, of the act. Eating is another opportunity to put meditation into practice in our daily lives, in what we might refer to as ordinary moments. It's essential for us to remember that spiritual practice does not just happen during our daily meditation or if we are on retreat. We will want to embrace each occasion as it arises. At a meditation retreat, each meal is a practice in mindful eating. One is encouraged to eat in silence and, most of all, not to rush through a meal unconsciously. Instead one should chew the food and savor every bite in order to be with each bite as it takes place.

A popular exercise on retreat is the eating of a single raisin. We let the raisin become the object of our meditation, and it becomes our teacher. We begin by holding one raisin. We feel the texture of it in our hands, we smell it, and we explore our anticipation of eating it.

We slowly put the raisin in our mouths, letting it rest on our tongue. This single raisin alerts our taste buds, and they come alive.

We sit and note all that is going on by this simple act of resting a raisin upon our tongue. Next, we begin to chew this small morsel of food, which stimulates the senses to an even greater degree. We let our chewing be deliberate and eat slowly and methodically. We continue to chew and finally swallow, feeling the raisin as it moves down our throats.

The eating of a single raisin on retreat can take five or ten minutes. Through this experience, much can be revealed about our personal relationship with food and eating. We find many things going on beneath the surface, independent of the act of eating, that usually don't surface in our sometimes-hurried pace of eating in our usual way.

Using eating as a meditation practice, we will want to offer our full presence to every meal, beginning with the preparation and serving of our food and culminating in the act of eating. Preparing our meal with loving kindness will permeate into the cells and nutrients of the food. We bring our awareness to the farmers who grew what we are about to enjoy and thank the universe for the sun and rain that participated in the birth of this meal.

In 1987, I spent a week at a spiritual community in northern Scotland called Findhorn. This progressive communal experiment became famous in the 1970s for growing gardens in a once-barren area. When not meditating or attending workshops, I worked in the kitchen preparing beautiful vegetarian meals. The residents and visitors practiced mindful eating in all aspects, from growing the food to preparing the food, and then eating in silence, mindful of each bite.

I remember a great lesson my first day in the kitchen making a salad for lunch. The head of the kitchen detail handed me all the ingredients, and among the different greens was a head of iceberg lettuce. My immediate comment was "What are we using this useless stuff for? It's mostly water." Wow! I was corrected immediately to such an extent that I found it necessary to make amends to the head of lettuce for saying that!

Everything we do with mindfulness is always motivated by loving kindness. Living life in all areas with mindfulness can bring one much happiness.

CHAPTER FORTY-FIVE

KARMA

"It wouldn't be happening if it wasn't supposed to happen." Karma is about what is happening in our lives right now, in this moment, and has everything to do with what actions and thoughts we engaged in before our current existence. In the simple teaching of mindfulness, we learn to embrace each moment as it is. If we understand and practice a belief in karma, then we know that at some point, somewhere, we ultimately arranged for this present moment to occur.

By accepting what is, we rid ourselves of blame while also freeing ourselves from the ricochet of our past. This is *radical acceptance:* that we will continue to get the teachings we need in order to crack open our hearts. The teachings come disguised as our lives, and every moment will provide us with exactly what we need to learn to open and awaken.

The concept of karma originated in ancient India; it is known as the cycle of cause and effect and death and rebirth. In the simplest and clearest definition, it means that what we set into motion comes back, or "what goes around comes around."

Karma is not to be considered a punishment or retribution, but it is an extended expression or consequence of our natural acts.

Conversely, through acts of love and service to others, we can create what is called *merit karma*. In the sacred Vedanta text the *Bhagavad-Gita*, Lord Krishna (the embodiment of the Godhead) speaks much of karma, of acting in a positive and dutiful regard, and then staying out of the results. The *Bhagavad-Gita*, chapter thirteen, verses twenty-seven to twenty-eight, says to me, "He who sees truly sees the Lord in much the same way in each and every creature, also sees the deathless in the hearts of all who die. Seeing the Lord everywhere, he does not harm himself or others." Krishna is ultimately describing remaining mindful of our thoughts, deeds, and the certain benefits of practicing merit karma in all facets of our lives. In twelve-step programs, there is a corollary to Step Three, "Let Go and Let God," and the recovery service maxim of "doing the right thing for the right reason."

Karma can also be an invitation to a belief in reincarnation. I began studying spiritual books while still using and before my earliest days of recovery; for me the 1960s countercultural revolution demanded the exploration of Eastern philosophies and religions. After getting clean and entering recovery, I was introduced early on to the wisdom of Edgar Cayce.

I read every book I could find written by Cayce or authors who wrote about him. Cayce is considered one of the greatest American psychics, and he became known as the "Sleeping Prophet." He would enter a trancelike state and answer questions about healing, reincarnation, and future events. Edgar Cayce's Association for Research and Enlightenment is located in Virginia Beach, Virginia, and all of his readings are on file in the center's library.

With my enthusiastic desire to study spiritual books with a leaning toward Eastern teachings, I soon began to gain a greater understanding of karma. It helped me to answer the questions of how a so-called loving God could let a young child grow up in a life of abject poverty, suffer ongoing abuse, or develop a fatal illness. What could such a child have possibly done to deserve such experiences?

This is where the belief in reincarnation began to soften my attitude and allow me to become more open and gain a greater comprehension of what the present moment seemed to mean as it encircled me, my life, and the lives of others. Horrific things that made no sense to my logical and intellectual mind began to diminish in a gradual, gentle way. The birth of new understandings began to give me a different insight from what had been perceived as a hostile universe to one that was now working for me and not against me. The law of karma opened my heart and mind, and I found that peace could prevail even within the most unacceptable circumstances. This new insight enabled compassion to replace my acrimonious and suspicious view of a vengeful God.

My first living spiritual teacher, Flobird, often referred to karma. One thing she emphasized repeatedly was that loving action can help burn up some of our karmic debt, and that our continued spiritual practice was in fact our defense against serving a life sentence due to past actions. It is quite understandable that living a life of mindfulness now assures us that our next moment will be one we wish to embrace fully. I started to understand that because the universe is loving, we can receive a pardon for good behavior. Flobird always reminded us to be grateful that we weren't held accountable for all bad karma we set into motion, contingent only on our willingness to grow spiritually, even while embracing our imperfections.

When it comes to my own personal life, I have no problem embracing the fact that I came here in this lifetime to embrace addiction and that the simplicity of it is that I was born this way.

I don't need to understand my biological makeup that might have contributed to my addictive personality. I'm completely at peace with the fact that my karma was set up before I got here and that by inviting all my unfinished business to this moment, this would be my path to continue the awakening of the spirit within.

Thoughts About Waking Up

Once the awakening begins, don't dwell
on how long you were asleep. What's important
are the moments that follow.

What I may call "the dark night of the soul"
can simply be my ideas of how life should unfold,
clouding the true vision.

I noted the green grass shimmering in the sun. It waved
to me as a breeze passed by; suddenly I was awake.

A devotion to a spiritual life is a life lived letting go.

If you are confronted by a situation where you have to
surrender or let go, don't feel alone. The spiritual path
sometimes demands this of us all. View it as an offering,
and let it call you to a deeper practice.

When the spirit awakens, don't hit the snooze
button and go back to sleep.

Always a decision: dwell in the past, worry about the
future, or rest in the wonderful moment, beautiful moment.

Meditation practice encourages a life
lived with less force.

The daily practice of mindfulness inspires a life
of accepting and embracing what is.

The invasion of a prevalent whisper may be heard,
convincing us that our challenges are different;
it is only the mantra of ego.

When indecision strikes, ask, “What would love do?”

Each moment spent in mindfulness is auspicious.

To awaken, pay attention (mindfulness)
to the moments of your life.

Warning: Meditation is for practice only . . .
please try at home.

No guru, no teacher: just you and
I practicing conscious breathing.

The way of the sage is to expect
nothing and accept what is.

Only when awake can we be touched by the suffering
of others. Send all sentient beings loving kindness.

A significant part of my practice is to keep returning
to the moment with the extraordinary realization:
If I can't be happy now, then when?

If I exclude my judgment of what is,
I can find joy in most experiences.

With one mindful breath, all stories about
past and future can fall away, and we're left
with our true nature—*joy*.

Let go of what you're not, and be
delighted with who you are.

Practice conscious breathing and you
will come to know the meaning of
present moment, wonderful moment.

Anytime, anywhere, I would love to sit with you.

I searched with enthusiasm for union with the divine,
and then suddenly I caught my breath; to my surprise,
the simplicity of the moment was the quest.

Practice radically for the sake of all sentient beings.

We look everywhere and finally look within.

Breathing with mindfulness will enable you to glimpse
the source breathing within you.

As the awakened person moves through life
with mindfulness, the gentle sound of conscious
breathing awakens still others.

The constant activity we engage in to hide from
suffering is why our search for joy seems unattainable.
Until we become still, we don't realize that what
we seek is hidden within.

As spirit awakens, our egos become more disabled.
Is yours nearing retirement?

Natural foods, exercise, and mindful eating will allow the body to adjust to its optimal weight.

If letting go doesn't work, try letting be.

Mindfulness meditation is the opposite of out-of-body meditation.

Meditation is our introduction to the space of *here* and the time of *now*.

A fleeting experience of intimacy with the moment can be the motivation to practice for eternity.

Whatever you're doing, know you're doing it, while you're doing it.

The silence we might feel on a summer evening while sitting along a mountain stream is but a glimpse of the silence we can find deep within.

Mindfulness asks us to be a part of life as it's happening.

The world has become incredibly small, so be kind to everyone.

CHAPTER FORTY-SIX

PRACTICING THE PRESENCE

The essence of this book and any of the spiritual practices that are available is to be able to practice the Presence. You can call it by any name that inspires you: God, true nature, the divine, higher self, or The Now.

If you are drawn to this book or any spiritual teaching, it is surely because you are searching for the missing link that binds you with your natural state of joy and peace. We are being drawn by a magnet to a life absent fear, separation, and discontentment. I believe that what we are longing for is a life where we attempt to practice Presence consciously in every moment of every day.

There is no need for a secret initiation into a cult that enables us to embrace a life of joyful living. One only needs to develop a spiritual awareness of being present and practicing the Presence. I have referred many times in the pages that have preceded this chapter to the joy one can find from this simple practice. When we embrace with delight what each moment offers, we can perceive the loveliness behind every action.

Brother Lawrence served as a lay brother in a Carmelite monastery in Paris, France. Christians commonly remember him for the intimacy he expressed concerning his relationship to God as recorded in a book compiled after his death, the classic Christian text *The Practice of the Presence of God.* Brother Lawrence worked in the kitchen of the monastery and spoke of washing the dishes while practicing the presence of God. Today one could call this "washing dishes with mindfulness." He found himself lost in the love of God while moving through his day in complete Presence even during the most commonplace and seemingly trivial chores. Brother Lawrence felt that being present with each task made every detail of his life possess unsurpassed value: "I began to live as if there were no one save God and me in the world." Brother Lawrence felt that he cooked meals, ran errands, scrubbed pots, and endured the scorn of the world alongside God. One of his most famous sayings refers to his mindfulness practice in his kitchen: "The time of business does not with me differ from the time of prayer; and in the noise and clatter of my kitchen, while several persons are at the same time calling for different things, I possess God in as great tranquility as if I were upon my knees before the Blessed Sacrament." This is the practice of mindfulness in action.

When people journey through life unconscious, they move though a typical day like a stampede of horses, missing what can be a delightful experience. When we awaken through mindfulness, and move through our lives, we rein in our ego and our desires, becoming present in the moment and finding joy in our own ordinary tasks. We allow the practice of mindfulness to be with us in every aspect of our lives.

As we arise from our morning meditation, we invite our awareness to continue to be with us and we surrender to becoming fully involved with what we are doing while we are doing it. This is practicing the Presence. When you move through your day with complete attention, you will hear and see spiritual teachings everywhere—even in the kitchen sink, washing dirty dishes.

Many times it may feel as though your mind is cluttered with more thoughts than there are moments. Please remember: The breath can be your anchor throughout the day. Just keep returning to it, and whatever you are pursuing, do it purposefully. This practice can cause much joy and peace in your life.

Practicing the Presence becomes a gentle occupation. While we're participating in the many areas of our lives and suddenly realize we are rushing through what we are doing, without judgment we return to the breath and slow down to the speed of the moment.

CHAPTER FORTY-SEVEN

OUT OF BODY

Out-of-body experience (OBE), also referred to as astral travel, astral projection, and soul travel, can be experienced through certain meditation techniques, which encourage this phenomenon.

Eckankar was founded by Paul Twitchell in 1965 and organized as a religious movement. One of the basic tenets of Eckankar is that the Soul (the true Self) can experience separation from the physical body in a state of full consciousness and travel freely into other planes of reality. This idea goes back to ancient times, when it was called astral travel.

Although there are meditation techniques used to induce this type of experience, it seems to occur as a spontaneous moment that happens without intent. The phenomenon that happens during an OBE is almost identical to what we hear from accounts of near-death experiences (NDE). When people explain these highly similar episodes, they generally describe the sensation of being detached from the physical body and "looking down" at themselves.

In my personal experience, this OBE phenomenon has always happened without any form of prior intention, methodology, or designated practice that would encourage this type of occurrence.

Curiously enough, it started happening during my first few months of surrendering to recovery and continued to occur many times in my first twenty years of not using. My earliest days of recovery also featured my experiencing many "flying dreams," which could be viewed as a reminder of the spirit being detached from the physical form.

What started to happen to me was quite scary and is a documented medical condition known as *sleep paralysis.* This paralysis would happen soon after I lay down for a nap, or when I went to bed. I would feel completely awake but at the same time feel paralyzed, as if I were in the grip of a powerful anesthetic. I could hear people talking, but I could not move. I wanted to snap out of it, and eventually I would be able to move a finger, which would then allow me to move my body.

Later, in my deepening studies of various spiritual books, I came upon some writings about OBEs and how to experience one. It described the sleep paralysis I had experienced, and it also assured the reader-aspirant that this feeling would occur. This sensation was the beginning of the spiritual body detaching from the physical body. The next time it came upon me, I just relaxed and surrendered to what happened. Suddenly, I found myself looking down at my physical body as I floated around the room. It was quite exhilarating, but my excitement seemed to end the experience, and I returned back into the body. One time I was lying in bed at night with my wife sleeping next to me and the feeling reappeared, so I just let it happen. I found myself rising up to a sitting position in the bed as I looked over and saw my wife sound asleep. I was so excited that I popped back into my body once again.

There are thousands of people who follow Eckankar and other practitioners who encourage pursuit of OBEs. Many techniques exist to help seekers transcend the thought process. For the last twenty years I have leaned toward the practice of mindfulness, which in most ways is the complete opposite practice of OBEs.

If anything, mindfulness, and Vipassana meditation in particular, encourages someone to use the body sensations as a vehicle into a deeper state of awareness. What I practice today is to be completely present with what is occurring in this moment and to not try to change it in any way.

Even in practicing mindfulness I've had what we might label as incredible experiences, none of which has been sought intentionally. I have seen my third eye, or spiritual eye, on many occasions. I have had what is called the kundalini experience, where pure energy rushes up the spine and awakens the chakra centers. *Kundalini* is a Sanskrit word meaning "coiled up like a snake."

There are therapists who specialize in kundalini massage therapy, chakra alignment, and energy work. Many systems of yoga focus on the kundalini awakening through meditation, breathing, and chanting of mantras.

Energy release and awakening of the chakras might happen while practicing meditation, but I assure you that they are not things we want to hang on to or lead us into thinking that we have reached some sort of transcendent consciousness. We haven't. If anything, one can attach to or find deep meaning in these sorts of admittedly powerful experiences, but they can tether us to the past rather than propel us into the present.

We must never limit ourselves to what we *think* is spiritual growth or attainment. What I strive for is to be in my body, in this moment, with complete awareness of what life is offering me right here, right now, and to put love into action, expecting nothing. When you can do that, you long for nothing else.

CHAPTER FORTY-EIGHT

PAINS OF SPIRITUAL GROWTH

I describe myself as an addict of the hopeless variety. This barely gives you a glimpse of the hell I experienced before entering recovery. I never want to return to using again and have remained willing to do whatever it takes each day to not use. I have not used and have worked my recovery for over forty-three years.

Having said that, I will say that I have hurt worse and felt more pain while living clean and being in a twelve-step recovery program than I did when I was using. One reason is obvious: the fact that I'm no longer able to anesthetize myself and numb my feelings. I have to face life on life's terms. Just the simple truth of having to grow up and not run away from problems explains a lot about the pain we must go through when we are new in recovery.

Like many addicts, I thought that once I stopped using, all of this insanity and obsessive thinking in my mind would vanish. However, the reality was, as it is with so many addicts in recovery, that it was my first glimpse into the real face of addiction, realizing that using was just a manifestation and symptom of a deeper and insidious disease. This was an adult dose to take, yet it was also the beginning of my spiritual awakening.

I believe the main contributor of this kind of unforeseen, unimaginable, and surely uninvited pain is the reality that I had stepped onto the spiritual path. I began the deep kind of inquiry required of meaningful twelve-step work and also started to practice meditation daily.

My first spiritual teacher, Flobird, called it "pains of spiritual growth," the idea that we were going through a body change, meaning that our old self was dying and we were becoming spiritualized. Flobird explained to me that when the old self is beginning to fade away, it is like the crucifixion of the false self. The rebirth of the spiritual self can sometimes be extremely painful, and the resistance from the ego can become a battle waged solely within.

In my previous book, *The Mindful Addict*, I referred to the last forty years of Mother Teresa's life. After she died, they found her personal journals, which revealed that she had quite a battle with feeling separated from her God. However, her life remained dedicated to serving others. Flobird emphasized this very practice and spiritual truth many times: No matter how we feel, we must continue to be of loving service, and we must persist in serving others.

The Spanish mystic Saint John of the Cross wrote in great detail about the journey the soul must take from its bodily home to its union with God. This Roman Catholic saint called this painful excursion "The Dark Night of the Soul." Even in contemporary Christianity, the term "dark night of the soul" is used to define a kind of spiritual crisis, which most sincere travelers will inevitably experience once they embark on this spiritual path.

I've said before that I believe the spiritual road is essentially paved with paradoxes. The pain we can experience because of our commitment to a spiritual practice is worthy of being called a paradox. This discipline sets into motion the beginning of what can be seen as a beacon pointing us toward the path; this beacon can manifest itself initially as a spiritual crisis. The practice can soften any challenges we are experiencing in our lives. This paradox can cloud our thoughts as we try to figure out why our spiritual growth can be what draws the "dark night" to us and at the same time eases us through it. When we embrace the spiritual life, in a sense we begin to die. It's the death of the ego or false self. This death is in fact our entrance into a higher calling or deeper practice. As we leave behind all that we hung on to for security and happiness, things fall away. We are called to walk away from what we thought would bring us joy.

We muddle the question of why we are here, and we're told to learn to love unconditionally. When in pain, we seek help from our spiritual advisors, and they say that putting love into action is the way to get out of the ego. There are days when it becomes so dark that we can't even pray, and we're told that our hearts are being stretched to accommodate more love. The answer is always about love.

Meditation practice brings us much joy and peace. Many times this calming wisdom comes in the form of hindsight, after we have walked through a difficult challenge and we can then see the whole picture: an image of awareness, which we could never have perceived while in the midst of our pain. Then again, almost paradoxically, we realize that if these problems or challenges had not occurred, we wouldn't be where we are today. It is through adversity that we are able to truly grow.

Meditation practice also helps us to discern what we are feeling. The longer we have practiced, the more we become cognizant of what is actually going on within. Something may feel out of place, and then we begin to see that what we are feeling is the suffering of others. As we start to awaken within, our hearts begin to open. Our practice is training us to be spiritual warriors, and we are beginning to cross over an invisible line. We are becoming more open to becoming a channel of assistance and service to others on this path. In the Buddhist tradition, this is called becoming a bodhisattva. We now fully realize that our lives are not our lives; the spiritual warrior is emerging, and there is no turning back.

Our new gig is to now be mindful of all sentient beings and to help heal all suffering on the planet. Now we take no thought for ourselves, and we put others first. Like Mother Teresa, we can't afford to dwell on the pains of our own spiritual growth; we are concerned only with the pains of another's spiritual evolution.

CHAPTER FORTY-NINE

THE INNER LIFE

The spiritual path will continue to lead us within. The paradox is that by practicing mindfulness, we are asked to pay close attention to the physical world as we move through it. We start each day on our meditation cushion and acutely observe all that is going on, observing our thoughts and feelings that rise and fall. We notice any body sensations as they appear. We don't try to block any sounds, but rather allow them to come to us as another element of meditation.

We are asked to notice everything without passing judgment on what occurs, even after our formal meditation sitting has ended. Regardless of how long we decide to sit each day in formal meditation, the time we spent sitting is really preparing us for the remaining hours of each day.

Over time we begin to notice the impermanence of everything from our feelings, relationships, and experiences to even our perspective toward material objects. It becomes clear that our suffering is from attaching to or avoiding what each moment presents. We begin to notice that our inevitable suffering can be softened through grace and acceptance; above all else, this embracing of reality ultimately drives us to look within. Provided with this emerging insight, we begin to adopt an inner life; this decision is the beginning of our journey within, as we shed our agendas, attachments, and resistance to the material world.

This is the highest calling, and it is where our intellect and spiritual self experience union. We find ourselves awake and embracing each moment and are amazed with what is before us. Obstacles now become opportunities for growth. Grace grants us a glimpse where each moment holds a sacred spot to find rest.

During this awakening, we use our spiritual eyes to see things as they really are and find ourselves content to live each day without any agenda. Suddenly, we know and understand that everything is about being present.

We begin to listen in silence to a wordless form of guidance, finding ourselves directed to our true and most comforting destination. In our realization of this precious moment, mindfulness compels us to let go of any judgments, persuading us to completely surrender to what it is offered. Each moment has the seed of inspiration that can free us from the self-made prisons of our minds, open our hearts to love, and enable us to grow in healthier ways.

Many people have spent their entire lives looking only for material fulfillment. They gather more material items around them in order to try to hold on to some ever-shifting sense of security. If they are fortunate, the suffering and discontentment of this never-ending venture will win out; with complete abandon, they will close their eyes and choose to look within.

Those who have gone before us, both in the practice of mediation and in the realm of recovery, teach us that we can find tremendous relief from our suffering if we let these realizations return us to the sense of direction that is received only from within. Being filled with grace, that ineffable solace that exists inside us all, is the purest way to explain the process of delving into the depths of our inner life.

As we accept this interior invitation and view the divine as the true self, we begin to understand the importance of a continuing practice. We can learn to realize that this love, our true nature, is always available and actually seeks us out as we inhale and exhale each mindful breath. Each time we return to our breath or interior life, it sets into motion a kind of death to our exterior or false self. We bury our past to become reborn into our present. We are continually reminded that the spiritual path calls on us to let go and surrender in each wonderful moment.

CHAPTER FIFTY

SPIRITUAL PRINCIPLES

We all have principles that we live by. In many cases, we are unconscious of them—but they show up in the ways that we move through our lives and conduct our affairs. *Principle* means a fundamental proposition or truth that serves as the foundation for beliefs or actions. Too many in the world's population embrace principles that tend to be concerned with the protection of themselves: putting themselves first above all else. Many people will do anything it takes to get ahead in the world of business or nurture their desire for power and prestige. Their ongoing motivation is to acquire more, anything and everything to shield and protect one's self from the fear of not having enough, not getting what they think they deserve, or never measuring up to an ever-shifting standard of success or acclaim.

The day comes for some of us when we strive to be happy, secure, and peaceful—using wavering and compromised principles that have been orchestrated by our own egos—until we discover how we seek to achieve success is a totally ineffective way to continue to live our lives. We "hit bottom" in trying to climb up a rickety ladder of success. This newly found awareness forces us to walk with a new attitude and to replace our ego-driven principles with principles that are inherently spiritual in their nature.

Every religion has principles. They are put in place to encourage a life wherein we surrender our ego-based false selves and begin to live a life where our actions will be more centered on service to others. Once you step upon the spiritual path (it doesn't matter which religion or spiritual practice you are drawn toward), the path will contain directions on how to live. The principles that we start to adapt and live by are like signposts along the road that give us directions. If they are followed to the best of our ability, we will begin to notice a profound personality change taking place.

Christians have the Ten Commandments; they encourage a standard of living that promotes an intimate relationship with the God of their understanding. Buddhism is centered on the Four Noble Truths, the fourth of which is referred to as the Eightfold Path. I cover this in greater detail in Chapter Sixteen, if you wish to refer back to it. Muslims follow the Qur'an, which contains the teachings to be followed in the Islamic, or Muslim, tradition.

In defining *Muslim*, the Sufi mystic and spiritual teacher Ibn Arabi said: "A Muslim is a person who has dedicated his worship exclusively to God." *Islam* means "making one's religion and faith directed toward God alone."

I asked a friend who is Muslim about this belief, and he stated this as "the One Straight Path. We pray for it every day." The Straight Path is explained in the first verse of the Holy Qur'an and is as follows: "Guide us to the Straight Way. The Way of those on whom You have bestowed Your Grace, not (the way) of those who earned Your Anger, nor of those who went astray."

Among other similarities, one shared universal aspect of these and all other religions, wisdoms, and philosophies is that they are founded on principle. In the area of recovery, we have the Twelve Steps, and each step contains many spiritual principles.

Agnostics and atheists alike can recover using the Twelve Steps because they are not expected to believe in a certain God or practice any particular faith; they can recover from addiction if they practice certain spiritual principles, which are universally accepted truths or guides to living a good and healthy life.

To be completely effective and to enjoy our journey along the spiritual path, we must do more than read the written words on these various signposts. We must embrace these principles and make them our fuel for moving through our daily lives. Only then will these fundamental, positive truths and subsequent actions be able to ignite any kind of change within us. I think the closing passage of Step Twelve explains this with much accuracy: "We practice these principles in all our affairs."

In other words, we are not just sitting in our place of worship or a meeting room, but rather in the context of our whole lives we try to practice a principled life each and every day and in each and every situation. Through the practices of prayer and meditation, which are disciplines of most spiritual paths or religions, we eventually begin, one moment at a time, to allow our egos to retire as the bosses of our lives.

There are countless principles that one can discover only after committing to a spiritual practice. You will start to acquire or become mindful of new ways to walk through life and sustain that very same loving and peaceful approach. The way the ego recedes is to replace the questionable principles that have been ingrained in us with newer ones that come to us through our spiritual quest.

A few examples of principles that you will find yourself living by include surrender, hope, acceptance, faith, trust, courage, honesty, forgiveness, love, equanimity, impermanence, service, humility, tolerance, nonjudgment, compassion, and mindfulness. The list goes on, and it will grow as you grow inside. When these principles are accepted, embraced, and then practiced, our lives begin to change dramatically, and the profound personality change will be transformative and ongoing.

CHAPTER FIFTY-ONE

MEDITATION PREPARES US

This book has been about living life in the moment, which is the experience of living our lives to the fullest. When we are not present, life is literally passing us by. After all, The Now is all there is. Yet our minds are preoccupied with thoughts of the past and future. Such thoughts, by their very nature, become a complete distraction from what is really happening.

Meditation practice is what prepares us to embrace what is and to live in the here and now. If disciplined seekers are serious about staying present and surrendering to each passing moment, then they will find themselves practicing mindfulness throughout their entire lives.

Many who practice meditation see it not only as a preparation for being present *now*, but also to prepare for being present during the inevitability of dying. In the Hindu religion, a guru—a realized yogi (man) or yogini (woman)—who has attained the state of enlightenment will, at the appropriate time, consciously exit the body. This is known as *mahasāmdhi*. The guru goes into a deep meditation as the end of his or her earthly life nears, and the transition becomes a culmination of his or her meditation practice in this lifetime. We may not be great gurus, but our daily practice can guide us from within, where we can experience the eternal silence. It is a place that can enable us to experience our transition with total grace and to die with complete dignity.

Through the practice of meditation, we spend our lives learning to be conscious or to be fully awake, which means to be fully alive. In the past quarter century, the Western world has thankfully enjoyed a movement and shift in consciousness where death has become a topic discussed in the open rather than something to be feared. People like Stephen and Ondrea Levine, Raymond Moody (who has written crucial books regarding near-death experiences, or NDEs), and Elizabeth Kübler-Ross have brought the topic from the darkness into the light.

Hospice has become available throughout the United States and the United Kingdom, providing compassionate care and support for both the dying and their families. Many times the patient is able to die at home. Through a blending of fear-based belief systems, a seemingly cultural awkwardness toward the dying, and surely an almost-encouraged sense of denial, death has been a longtime taboo subject in the Western world. Consequently, it is looked upon as something that we should fear. Death is something family members don't know how to talk about; we seem to talk around our deaths. However, hospice volunteers sit with the dying person and are available to talk about this experience with the soon-to-be-deceased; these same volunteers are also trained and prepared to talk openly with the family.

This ongoing movement, addressing death and dying, has helped the Western world to emerge from the darkness of denial and pain and has allowed us to walk into the light of openness and solace. Today there are many people, because of their ongoing meditation practices and the directness toward this universal reality, who are dying in a surrendered state with their minds and hearts open. A sense of peace can be felt by many in the room where a person makes this final life transition. Grief eventually becomes a gift, another paradox of a life centered on the spirit.

Sadly, many still live in a state of confusion and a life of fear; this kind of accumulated dread can follow them right into their moment of death. There is nothing easy about this process, but it can become a gentler journey for anyone who begins a spiritual discipline; to practice being present while living follows us into the moment of our death.

Right now, in this very moment of our lives, we practice embracing everything that life might surprise us with, including dying, as each moment gently unfolds. As we contemplate death and practice becoming more accepting and even friendlier with it, we see that life and death are one and the same. One cannot exist without the other. Life and death are the ultimate Alpha and Omega.

In the Gnostic scripture "The Gospel of Thomas," Jesus Christ assures his disciples in Logion 18 the following: "Where the beginning is, the end will be." Everything must come to an end so that we can have a new beginning, a kind of universal resurrection of spirit that is fired by love, not fear. The process for each of us is merely the passage of our spirit to its next adventure that encourages our awakening.

If we fear life, we will surely fear death. If we are living our lives consciously, we will in turn embrace our deaths and die consciously. During the process of dying, our friends and family will have a tendency to follow our lead. If we hold a place within that is of peace, acceptance, and surrender, and we embrace the principles of impermanence and equanimity, we will be setting the atmosphere for them as well. If we embrace the adventure with love, there will be nothing but love in the room, and any fears will be dispelled by this very same love.

As our spiritual quest deepens, the wisdom both revealed and attained can be used to prepare for death. If we find meaning in each moment, every moment becomes an opportunity. We experience an absence of fear and embrace our inevitable adventure of life and death, seeing it as a unified whole.

In Tibetan Buddhism, the concept of the bardos (translated as "intermediate states") is a key belief that is described as the transitional states between incarnations, or lives. Sogyal Rinpoche writes eloquently about his views on the bardos in his acclaimed book *The Tibetan Book of Living and Dying*. Rinpoche explains these transitions by saying that a bardo is like the moment when a master introduces a disciple to the essential and innermost nature of the mind. The moment of death is the greatest and most charged of these moments.

Through our practice of meditation, we can experience what is described as the Four Bardos during our meditation. This is a way of introducing someone to what is explained as the journey of our spirit during and after death. The bardos are as follows:

- The first bardo is the natural one of life.
- The second bardo is the process of death and dying.
- The third bardo is after death, the luminous bardo.
- The fourth bardo is rebirth, the karmic bardo of becoming.

Through my own practice of meditation and my attempt to live by spiritual principles, I can honestly say I have no regrets about my life. I hope to carry this awareness to my last moments in this body and be conscious of having no regrets when it is time for my transition. Death can be a joyful conclusion to a life lived to the fullest.

CHAPTER FIFTY-TWO

THINGS ARE NEVER WHAT THEY SEEM

Our journey down the spiritual path has a way of encouraging us to keep shedding the self that we think we are. By practicing mindfulness, we begin to see that when we are in the present moment, we cannot be in the midst of a story line, which is the endless stream of thoughts that we seem to blindly follow. When caught up in this continuous deluge of false consciousness, our lives become a fictitious illusion, a fable, produced by a hallucinatory mind. It seems so real that we actually feel stress over something that hasn't even happened, and we live in the fear of things we can't even identify. We become convinced that the separateness we experience is all too real. Once we take the first committed step on the spiritual path, we begin the adventure of shedding the skin of what we are not, and returning within to what we truly are.

I suggest to people in twelve-step recovery that the disease of addiction is when we are driven by our fear and the separateness that we have felt our entire lives.

Conversely, recovery is about finding intimacy within ourselves and, eventually, with the outside world. The practice of insight meditation is where we start to become friendly with our thoughts. We learn not to attach, but to simply note our busy minds, not letting our fleeting thoughts and body sensations become magnets that pull us back into the story line. This is the beginning of seeing things as they are, casting off our false ideas of ourselves and the world. When we allow ourselves to become friendly with our thoughts and begin to see new things surfacing beneath our old ideas of who we thought we were, we begin to see our situation as more friendly. Consequently, unnamed and irrational fears begin to dissolve.

We begin to reflect on our lives and the challenges we have been through. With hindsight, we observe that we have never really solved any of our problems. We disguise our problems by masking them with attachment and avoidance. Life has a way of coming together and then falling apart. That is the very nature of impermanence. Like the thoughts we observe and experience during meditation, life situations come and go. What was real one moment falls away and is gone.

This insight is what reveals the truth in how things really are. We have developed this idea that we can overcome a problem, but the truth is that we never really solve anything because it falls apart before we can. The dual phenomena of experience and time just keep re-forming and dissolving, again and again.

Seeing things as they truly are is putting equanimity into action. We just have to create a space in our lives to notice how things continually come together and then collapse, over and over again.

Equanimity is the key to help us unlock the door that imprisons us in trying to judge and label our experiences as they unfurl. Living a life of mindfulness is not about constantly feeling a heavenly glow or existing in a place that is going to be lovely all the time. When looking at my own experience, while seeking a spiritual path on these terms, I discover that how I view and participate in the world is what has caused me the most suffering.

Believing that we will find continuous pleasure and avoid pain is a trap; it is this unrealistic desire that causes many people to lock themselves into a life of suffering. It is a worldview focused on fulfilling constant, shape-shifting expectations. There is a humorous, yet certainly true, recovery maxim that assures us, "Expectations are like premeditated resentments." I tell people whom I sponsor in twelve-step recovery to avoid looking for a gold star next to their name, with the illusion that they will never hurt again. Once our spiritual awakening begins, it opens our hearts, and we start to feel everything as it should be.

We can't avoid the paradoxes because they're part of living and applying mindfulness to every moment. We move through life observing, but not attaching, and just this simple action will begin to soften each moment. After we've walked though each challenge, we find more joy by surrendering to what is instead of what should be.

The First Noble Truth of the Buddha tells us that suffering is inevitable for human beings as long as we continue to believe that things last, that they don't disintegrate, and that they can be counted on in any way to satisfy our security.

We improve our lives when we see things as they truly are, as we continue to work the Twelve Steps, or continue to follow the Four Noble Truths the Buddha offered in his initial teachings. We continue to walk whatever spiritual path we have chosen. By practicing spiritual principles, we will begin waking up, and it will be as though someone flipped a light switch. Once illuminated, we can then truly see that life is always in transition. The only reality we can count on is what is happening as it occurs in each moment. And that is the very nature of reality.

CHAPTER FIFTY-THREE

LOOKING FOR A SPIRITUAL TEACHER

The 1960s not only gave us the beginnings of the New Age movement, which blossomed within the flower power of hippie culture and love-ins, but most importantly, the era provided us with an emergence of Eastern teachings appearing in the West.

Prior to this, the word *guru* (spiritual teacher) was not a familiar term in the West. The stories of gurus were suddenly heard in daily conversations among the flower children. One of the first few teachers whose teachings were being explored was Paramahansa Yogananda. While Yogananda arrived in America in the early 1920s, his acceptance really began to flourish during the 1960s.

Because of The Beatles, Maharishi Mahesh Yogi became extremely popular and helped spread the practice of Transcendental Meditation (TM). With few spiritual teachers available in the 1960s, these two men were considered authentic gurus. In the early 1970s, a few Westerners who had journeyed through India returned with their experiences of discovering insight meditation, what has become known as "mindfulness."

If you're looking for a spiritual teacher, there is no shortage in today's market. Whether you're looking for a dharma teacher who practices the teachings of the Buddha or a guru who teaches the principles of the Hindu-based Vedanta, you will find our world seemingly flooded with spiritual teachers.

I think the problem isn't finding a teacher, but rather finding one who resonates within the vibration of your heart. One is surely best suited to follow the guidance of a teacher who is authentic, yet most of all one who is adamant that your questions are ultimately answered from within. A worthy teacher will live life by example and encourage you to put those teachings into action. If they are humble and sincere, they will assure you that enlightenment cannot be attained simply by sitting in the presence of one who is enlightened. The recurring message is that there is no softer way; we must live the principles in our own lives to ignite the flame of our own truth and enlightenment.

I was fortunate to meet a living and awakened being when I came into a twelve-step program. I felt so much grace living near and traveling with Flobird for ten years. Even now, over thirty years after her passing, the spiritual seeds she planted in my heart are still blooming as understandings and clarity about my path. These adventures and teachings are documented in my book *The Mindful Addict*.

The gift that practicing mindfulness meditation has given me is the simplicity of my breath becoming my mantra, and now the present moment has become my ultimate teacher. When we try to pay attention to each moment, it contains the very messages we need in order to grow toward our true nature—our enlightenment.

Once we start to embrace and lean into each moment, not trying to change what it offers, we begin to see that we don't have to create situations that we think will be beneficial to our growth. By our sitting with what we think is pleasant and unpleasant, and not pushing it away or denying anything that comes up, this uncomfortable process encourages our hearts to become open. As we develop from within, we receive insight into how we relate to life and the many situations and opportunities that we encounter each day. The spiritual growth occurs when we don't turn to any kind of addiction or negative behaviors to soften the razor's edge we seem to be standing on.

Meditation practice is an invitation to sit with each moment and notice how we get carried away by a promise of hope or a projection of fear. By sitting in the moment and observing all that is rising and falling, we begin to see how we react to our emotions and feelings. We realize through this experience that we can let go with every conscious breath. Our spiritual journey calls us to go beyond our fears and hopes, and many times this requires stepping into the unknown.

In my experience, the unknown is the inevitable destination of the spiritual path. When we walk upon the razor's edge, it is comparable to living our lives in a groundless world with nothing to hang on to and nowhere to turn. These are the moments that contain the true teachings. No matter how big or small the challenge, the lesson is to surrender to the discomfort of life and see it more clearly. We embrace it, sit with it, and refrain from returning to the illusion of relief sought through grasping, distraction, or even addiction.

This is the road to becoming a spiritual warrior. You might seek out or you might already have a spiritual teacher, but when we face the moment and the challenges it brings, the real teachings begin. These opportunities reveal themselves in ways we least understand, yet they are the sincere way to our true nature.

Each moment will always be the perfect teacher. The present moment is always with us and brings with it profound instructions. This belief is mentioned repeatedly within the pages of this book. And the simple act of paying attention to what is happening now is the spiritual practice. This is the teaching of mindfulness.

CHAPTER FIFTY-FOUR

DON'T TAKE IT PERSONALLY

Spiritual practice offers us an important lesson, and it is a teaching that leads us to a greater freedom within. It's incredibly simple: "What you think of me is none of my business." The thoughts that drift so frequently through my mind about me are even more consequential. These also are none of my business.

The inner judgments that stream through our consciousness are probably the hardest self-imposed verdicts to let go. We are caught off guard by our own thoughts, and not only do we pay too much attention to them, but we actually believe them to be true. There is a huge step toward our personal freedom when we realize we don't have to take this inner dialogue seriously. If we do not recognize this fact when we get caught up in the constant deliberation about who we are and what we think is happening, that inner dialogue will soon turn into one of our story lines. We have seen from our past experience that when we follow the directives of our mind, the outcome of being a participant in this kind of internal mania has no happy ending.

We must keep our security system activated at all times. To be on guard is to keep our observation functioning, by observing and not attaching to or avoiding our experiences. As long as we don't attach, we can stay clear of the madness at play.

The flip side of the coin is our pressing concerns about what others think of us. In our daily lives, we generally encounter a myriad of different personalities we inevitably will need to navigate through with hopefully some kind of civility and friendly communication. I think we've all had the experience at one time or another, when circumstances have required us to be in the public eye and possibly come under scrutiny. Perhaps we are obligated to deliver a business or work-related presentation or make a personal statement; in most cases, we are shown appreciation and support, and receive positive feedback from many people. It usually only takes one unkind remark, or even a simple statement that opposes our beliefs, to immediately spin us into a form of amnesia where we forget the many people who sincerely love and support us. We focus on the one negative response. In this process we allow one thought to take hold of us, and soon we believe and project the worst-case scenario.

If we're always looking for applause and acknowledgment, we will find ourselves disappointed daily. Our sitting practice teaches us to avoid clinging to what is pleasurable and not flee from feelings that are uncomfortable. We need to bring the practice of our meditation into our everyday lives. Most of us have a tremendous support group, either with our sangha or with our twelve-step recovery meetings. In the Buddhist tradition, the sangha is the community of monks and nuns or people who follow the teachings, the same as a congregation in the Christian church. Whereas, the twelve-step community refers to its support group as the fellowship.

We are loved and at times even praised and encouraged, but living by the principle of equanimity, we just let both the praise and the rejections pass by us. Until we come to believe that what others think of us is none of our business, we will continue to be trapped, grasping at or resisting what is in front of us.

What happens when we sit for meditation is our blueprint for mapping our way through each day. We are learning to walk the middle path between clinging to and running away from the impermanence of reality. We continue to observe and acknowledge what appears in our thoughts without judgment, and to our amazement our thoughts and life situations dissolve without our help. The act of getting out of our own way actually makes the way to live even easier. By this practice, we invariably return to the present moment.

We learn to do this in meditation and it permeates our busy lives. Suddenly we discover that we are not struggling as much as we used to as we learn to relax and embrace equanimity. Thoughts will still find their way in, and we will still latch on to opinions others might have of us, but we will begin to see our internal story line sooner and be able to drop this false narrative before it consumes us. This is where our openness will come from: letting go of what others think of us and coming back to the wonderful moment, beautiful moment.

I Was Thinking

The practice of mindfulness will let you see the ordinary as extraordinary.

Confusion is the ego's way of silencing communication with divine nature; just breathe, and know you're breathing. Listen to the silence.

Meditation is about nondoing with moment-to-moment awareness; it's best to sit with no goals or expectations. Many beneficial side effects can occur, one being our ability to embrace what life offers with equanimity.

Suddenly an event occurs that causes such an innocent joy to arise, seeming so sacred that I wonder why I can't hold it for eternity. Impermanence whispers to me, and I return to the moment and enjoy.

We all live in the same time zone, The Now.

While you are practicing mindfulness meditation, anything that pulls your attention from the breath is a distraction. We learn to observe the distraction mindfully and return to the breath; being someone who has practiced daily for many years, it seems I have done this a million times. Distractions have no power; by our observing and returning to our breath, they fade away.

Thoughts that go unobserved can hold us hostage.

Amnesia is common in the wake of the many challenges
that confront us daily; suddenly, as if by grace,
the forgetfulness vanishes, and I'm pleasantly reminded
that my tribulations are what propel me toward
the awakening of spirit.

Found the most awesome place to live:
the present moment, wonderful moment.

The part of you that observes stress does not feel stress.

With our comings and goings, we're just seeking
union with our true nature. Once awake, we see
no reason to be doing this and that.

Our contentment is found in nondoing,
practicing mindfulness breathing.

Don't just do something; sit there.

Meditation practice introduces you to noble silence,
where vocabulary becomes an interruption.

The mind wanders without effort, mindlessly grasping
for security at objects of impermanence. Becoming so
agreeable to dwell in the past and future, while looking for
applause and moving through life unconsciously: This is
the simplicity of suffering. Suddenly we catch our breath,
freeing us from the command of ego, and gently return to
the moment; the call to practice awakens us again.

While home alone, I am drawn to the meditation room. With mindfulness, I light candles and incense. Gently striking the Tibetan singing bowl, I sit purposely with each breath; suddenly I enjoy the silence, like a bit of afternoon delight.

While sitting in the stillness, I become mindful that I'm part of the energy that creates everything.

Our natural tendency is to seek security; we want and expect permanence. Within the beauty of our being, we notice again and again that there is nothing to hold on to; eventually we embrace impermanence.

I'm preparing for a thirty-day meditation retreat in a cave in the high peaks of the Himalayas; I'm having trouble finding one with Wi-Fi access.

The simplicity of the dharma is to stop the stories, stop the internal dialogue, and embrace the present moment. What's happening in life now is the vehicle to awaken.

The simplicity of meditation is that it doesn't matter if you have been practicing for decades or are just beginning. When you sit, all kinds of stuff arises. Do not repress it or cling to it; just acknowledge it. Soon it dissolves, and you return to the freshness of the present moment again and again.

As human beings, our potential is limitless; when following the dharma, we practice accepting what life offers now. Life's direction unfolds without force or manipulation. Without knowledge of what the next moment will bring, we find a gentle movement as we breathe and the dharma reveals our karma.

When addiction enters our lives, either through our own use or that of a family member, it can cause enormous confusion and pain and turn life, as we know it, upside down. The spiritual path of the Twelve Steps is not always easy, but the willingness to practice the steps will begin to soften our attitude toward addiction. Compassion and understanding will begin to fill the void that anger and resentment used to occupy. As we witness our lives and those around us change, we begin to see that our greatest challenges are often our introduction to a deeper compassion, engendering our view of life with a new sense of vision.

I find it futile to follow the bliss my mind perceives as such; instead I follow my breath, which leads to my true nature.

I find time travel to either the past or the future quite exhausting; I prefer to rest in the present moment.

Each moment contains many wonderful things; always remember that God is loving you now.

Challenges are announcements of something better to come.

As you sit and observe what arises, regard these thoughts and feelings with equanimity, compassion, humor, and an open heart. This attitude will become a paradigm shift in your daily life as uninvited challenges announce themselves.

CHAPTER FIFTY-FIVE

SIX WAYS TO OPEN OUR HEARTS

Flobird, my first spiritual teacher and sponsor, who introduced me to twelve-step recovery in 1968, was what the Buddhist tradition calls a bodhisattva. A bodhisattva is someone who has committed him- or herself to a life of service and compassion, one who has awakened and has chosen to serve and help others through their own suffering until they experience their own awakening. Flobird was what I call an authentic teacher; she taught the people who were fortunate enough to be around her through her words and actions. She lived the principles of the Twelve Steps, principles that are common for all true spiritual paths and that lead to the awakening of spirits and hearts.

My time spent with this remarkable woman was from 1968 until her passing in 1978. This time frame was before the popularity of mindfulness permeated the Western world, and yet, as I look back, we were living the dharma without naming it as such.

We were told that we were being trained to be world servers (bodhisattvas), and that to do this we had to become spiritual warriors. A genuine teacher, or spiritual path followed, will have similar principles that would benefit anyone who chooses to take the journey to enlightenment.

In the Buddhist teachings, there are six paramitas (principles), which will train you to live a compassionate life: generosity, discipline, patience, joyful exertion, meditation, and unconditional wisdom. I witnessed Flobird live these principles each day. No matter what was happening in the outside world, I watched her practice these principles without hesitation.

Through practice, we are introduced to a path that will take us beyond aversion and attachment, beyond self-obsession, and beyond the story line that says we are separate.

In the teachings of the dharma, these aforementioned principles are called the six *paramitas*, a Sanskrit word meaning "gone to the other shore." When we practice at this level, we begin to become comfortable with what each moment offers, and our lives start to have a freer and groundless quality. We begin to acknowledge the flow of impermanence and the fact that there is nothing to hang on to. We start to embrace the idea that our only security lies in the present moment.

As I look back, I can see the benefit of living around Flobird. She was awakened and was, without question, a great and rare gift. I could read and study all I wanted from a book, but to be immersed in on-the-job training with a genuine holy person was the catalyst for my own awakening to begin. Of the six teachings, the unconditional wisdom was of the utmost importance. With her wisdom, Flobird led us with gentleness along the spiritual path, as if she were guiding a blind person down a wooded trail.

She lived her life in a way that taught others to let go of thoughts of self, thoughts that were trying to convince us that we had a life to hold on to. Our natural instincts would be to protect ourselves and to hesitate stepping into what seemed like nothingness. Her loving kindness acted like a light that guided us each step of the way. We surrendered to her wisdom and made the leap of faith by letting go of the notion that we could hide in any corner and call it our own.

You felt her generosity, first of the paramitas, from the moment you met her; it exuded from her being. When we first see the word *generosity*, we think of giving away money or material things. This is an admittedly important aspect of this principle. My teacher had no material objects. She had no visible means of income. She had walked away from a life of having things to depend on. She truly lived in the moment and moved through life by following her heart, yet generosity was the essence of this holy woman. She gave her life away in each moment to anyone who entered it. At the deepest level, generosity is the spiritual metaphor of letting go. When we give away our lives, as in service to others or giving material possessions to benefit those who are without, what is really taking place at the level of the soul is that we are letting go of our own barriers, which create our separation from the precious moment at hand.

I have traveled through India on many occasions, and the opportunity to practice generosity is on every street corner. I enjoyed giving money to the poor who were begging on the street, but before giving money I sat down and made eye contact. I held my hands in the prayer position and said "Namaste," I touched them gently, and then, after making human contact, I gave them money. I saw how important each person truly was.

A good way to practice generosity is to look for opportunities in our lives each day. Give a smile to a stranger; if you visit a friend, bring a simple gift, such as a flower or a stick of incense. Generosity comes in all sizes, and any form of giving that is offered from the heart benefits others on some level.

Practicing generosity will immediately put us in touch with any resistance that has found a hiding place within. Becoming a spiritual warrior is training that we will be a part of for the remainder of our lives.

The six paramitas are here to continue to help guide us in becoming world servers. Anyone can talk the talk about how they live their spiritual path, but to actually walk the walk, to practice it when no one is watching, and to be authentic takes great discipline. Discipline is derived from the word *disciple*, and *disciple* is how I would describe myself in relationship to Flobird. Living and traveling with Flobird taught me the principle of discipline. Our covers were always pulled on us; we had to live this spiritual life; we couldn't just talk about it. Without discipline we cannot evolve on the spiritual path. To evolve means to change, hopefully for the better, and to change we have to practice each day, all day.

Learning to show up to meditation each day takes discipline: our simple technique of practicing mindfulness of our breath; to continue to watch and not attach to our thoughts; and the countless times during a thirty-minute meditation when we find ourselves lost in our story line and have to return to the breath. Without discipline, we wouldn't have a chance of returning to practice day after day. This type of discipline is not like military training where we become rigid with our practice, and it's not about being so relaxed that we fall asleep. We want to develop the technique of being present for all the moments of our lives.

During my early years in recovery, when I traveled with Flobird and a group of people, we would all come and go in and out of each other's lives. There seemed to be a core group of us who would be living in tents or mansions on the beach. We lived and traveled the path of groundlessness, never knowing where we would end up or how long we were going to be there. Since we were all new to the spiritual path, we had a lot of emotions surfacing all the time. Flobird seemed to always be resting in the abiding calm in the middle of everyone's chaos as we spun crazily in our own orbits.

We would each visit Flobird's room in the morning after meditation to share whatever seemed to be arising. One by one, we would file in and out, sharing our craziness each day. Flobird would sit there with a smile on her face every time I entered her room. She carried with her the next principle that is necessary on our path to enlightenment—patience.

Patience is the opposite of aggression. Our lesson was to learn to relax within the moment and what it offered us. Mindfulness teaches us to explore life in the present moment as it is occurring. I watched her do this day in and day out. She received people one by one, all day and every day, not only those of us who were living and traveling together, but the people who would come to this strange woman who had only unconditional love for anyone visiting. I think this is where the phrase "having the patience of a saint" came from. We must begin with ourselves; we learn in meditation while following our breath, and when we find our minds lost in thought, we learn to gently return to the breath. Being gentle in this way is patience. Patience allows us to rest in the moment with equanimity and wonder what each present moment offers us.

The next paramita or principle is joyous exertion. This is one of my favorites. As we continue our practice of mindfulness and service to others, our spirits continue to awaken and our hearts continue to open. As we become more comfortable living from one moment to the next, shedding our requirements to always know what's next and to always have to have outer security, we find ourselves living with more groundlessness. We start to feel joy emerge from within for no outer reason, and this joyful energy is what will keep us in awe of what each moment offers us.

In the early years with Flobird I often noticed that people could walk into a filled room, and when Flobird was in the room, without hesitation and with no preconditioning, they would be drawn to her because of the joyful energy that radiated from her. You didn't need a Geiger counter to pick it up; people were automatically drawn to her.

When people are in service, too much of the time it seems their service is ego-driven; there is no joy. But when we perform service and allow unconditional love to be our motivating force, we then will begin to feel this energy of joy arising from within. It can feel as though you will burst. This is the principle of joyous exertion in action: Our labor produces joy.

Our last paramita is meditation. What I have learned about meditation I found out early on while living and traveling with Flobird. It was the fuel that ignited her life. She started each day with about two hours of practice. It was as though everything she said or did and her every movement for the rest of the day were because of her morning practice. I witnessed her going around the world twice with no money at all. She lived in total groundlessness and emptiness, and she was spirit-guided in everything.

I understand that you may not have two hours a day to devote to practice and that you may not be able to travel the world with no money at this point in your life. But you would be surprised at what you *can* do when meditation becomes a consistent practice in your life.

In meditation we learn to sit and listen, and we learn to observe and not to manipulate. Meditation practice creates the space to let our awakening continue and to encourage our hearts to open. All six paramitas work together and are born from our continued meditation.

CHAPTER FIFTY-SIX

MEDITATION IS OUR ANTIDOTE FOR "*DIS*-EASE"

The "*dis*-ease" of our minds is mainly due to our tendency to battle against what life is offering us. We are addicted to struggle, strung out on resisting reality.

There are ways to decrease the stress and *dis*-ease we live with. Meditation encourages us to move toward, embrace, and let go of our difficulties rather than run away and deny they exist.

How long do we have to practice meditation to realize that what we call our struggles or challenges will continue to arise and then dissolve? The answer is forever, and we enter that eternity by returning to the present moment—more of the paradox that seems to fuel spirituality. We are reminded again and again that when we sit down to meditate, we do so with no agenda or goal to accomplish. It's about giving up our struggle to change anything; we merely practice relaxing with what is.

We soon notice that when we are talking about meditation, this discussion is repetitive, much like the actual practice of meditation.

We are reminded to keep returning to our breath and not attach to our story lines. The deeper we study and compare surviving wisdom traditions and paths to enlightenment, whether they are Buddhism, Vedanta, Islam, or the mystical edge of Christianity, we discover the recurring refrains of surrendering to silence and being fully present in the moment. In continuing a spiritual practice, we recognize that much of our stress or *dis*-ease is completely manufactured by our runaway thoughts, which are projecting some future catastrophic outcome. This is where the observation of "that which we resist, persists" resonates loudest. We just have to look at each moment that arises with a nonjudgmental attitude; this is what will bring our story line to "The End."

Once we stop writing, producing, directing, and watching the world premiere of the movie we screen in our minds, our projections into the future cease and showtime is over. Seeing things as they are and the continued repetition of practicing mindfulness are one method that helps our *dis*-eased minds find peace. Meditation practice is how we stop fighting with whatever situation we are in the middle of; we reach for the familiar principle of surrender and end our rebellion toward reality.

The second method is to practice using our difficulties as fuel to ignite our awakenings. I talked earlier about the technique of tonglen meditation. It's a form of service we can utilize while sitting in meditation. The method is to face what arises by embracing it. We purposely breathe in our pain and discomfort and absorb the suffering of others who are in similar situations. We use our discomfort to relieve their anguish, taking in the suffering of others as we inhale and exhaling loving kindness.

Putting others before ourselves is always a loving thing to do and redirects our self-centered thinking. We learn to look at any challenges that appear in our lives as a signal to dive deeper into our practice. Our daily practice of meditation begins to infiltrate our whole lives, and our once-frightening situations keep dissolving in front of us. Meditation continues to encourage us to move toward our difficulties.

In the practice of tonglen, the more we attempt this method, the greater ability we have to face those difficulties in the here and now. This may not make the challenges disappear, but they do soften as we find rest in the present moment. Remember that whatever is happening in this moment is our teacher, and our teachers always want to help us to awaken.

With continued practice of meditation, we become more relaxed with the way things are. This is why I call surrender one of the most important spiritual principles. Without surrender, we become stuck on the path of life. In picking our battles, we realize that the interior combat and war within never ends until we issue the cease-fire of mindfulness.

The next method is to see and treat whatever is happening as a blessing, a gift disguised as a challenge. As our story lines become shorter and shorter, losing their power to hold our attention with the dark mirage of impending disaster, our view of and reaction to life begin to change. First, we see what the teachings have been telling us all along: Life and the moment at hand are wonderful teachers. Shedding our ego-driven, catastrophic thinking, we soon realize that we could have never written a better scenario for our spiritual growth than the one offered by ultimate reality.

We see the universe or life in general as friendlier. Instead of being trapped with the idea that life is against us, we embark on a new journey where the universe is working in our favor.

After forty-plus years of consciously walking a path leading to love, I have adopted this motto for myself, and in difficult times I remember and embrace it: "God will take me in the ways I least understand for it to be the quickest." Every day I am convinced that I have no idea what is best for me and how to hasten my spiritual growth. I continue to rest in what the moment offers. May you live with ease.

CHAPTER FIFTY-SEVEN

MEDITATION IS ART

Each time we sit down to meditate, the discipline called for is similar to that of an author sitting down to write an award-winning piece of literature or a gifted painter whose artwork ends up in a museum. Meditation makes it possible for us to be guided in each moment to our highest calling, which is to be present. The way we travel through our daily lives, when we are following the guidance our hearts provide, is like creating a story that inspires others to listen to our tale or painting the most beautiful picture on our canvas. This is the art of meditation; this is the art of living in the moment.

What all great artists have in common is that they often refer to themselves as being a channel through which flows the finished product, as if it were something that seemed to have come through them. I once heard an interview with Richard Bach, the author of the international bestseller *Jonathan Livingston Seagull.* When asked how long it took to write this book, Bach responded that from start to finish, he spent ninety minutes writing this bestseller. Since the story had already been written within, Bach simply had to put pen to paper and let it out.

This defines how meditation was described to me in the beginning. We are to show up and sit; no transcendent experience is required. Although most people like experiences that are accompanied by feelings of rising above worldly concerns, this is not the purpose of meditation practice. In the purest form of practice, we are to sit and be willing to become a channel of compassion for all sentient beings.

We learn to listen within, discarding any personal agenda, and find our hearts opening as we are led to our highest good. Our practice of sitting each day is synonymous with the daily practice of any other kind of artist, whether it is a great musician or an all-star athlete: We continue to show up. Our daily practice is how we learn to gently maneuver our way through the game of life, one breath at a time.

The secret to the art of living life to the fullest is to stop demanding anything from the moment. As soon as we try to change or manipulate what is offered to us, we cease living in The Now. When we are not living in the moment, we are in a dream state. Living each day while practicing the Presence is living in The Now; it's what we call being awake. As soon as you drop your demands for how life should be, you suddenly find yourself in The Now.

Many times I will hear music that transports me to a place of inspiration, or I might gaze upon a photograph or a painting an artist has captured and become transfixed in that moment. This is where the path of meditation will lead us daily, by sitting and gazing within, or listening to the beauty of the silence that lies beneath our chatter. Our lives become a symphony of sound and sight while we are sitting on our meditation cushions, while we are doing nothing else except being still.

I start each day in the darkness of predawn; here I visit the inspiration within. This book and my first book were mostly written in the early hours of the day after sitting. I believe meditation is a catalyst that can ignite any of the arts. The paradox is that great music or a great painting can also be used to catalyze and ignite someone's meditation. Simply put, art encourages art.

Whether it's some form of meditation, hearing angelic music, or gazing upon a sunset, let the experience bring you back to The Now: May you touch the intrinsic loveliness of your true nature. To practice the art of meditation, we must continue to sit with the gift the moment gives us, with no demand to hang on or to remove anything, but to rest with what is.

Become the artist of your own life—practice daily and learn to work with what you have. As we continue to awaken, our vision clears, and we can see loveliness within ourselves and everywhere we look.

CHAPTER FIFTY-EIGHT

RENUNCIATION

The word *renunciation* carries with it a vision of joining a monastery, shaving our heads, donning robes, and possessing only our begging bowl. This, of course, is renunciation at the extreme attainment with the willingness to let go of all distractions and follow a disciplined spiritual path.

As many know who have embarked on a spiritual journey, once we are on the path, we are called to practice renunciation at different levels. The ongoing practice of letting go of our story lines is renunciation. I often mention to others that if you are going to begin a spiritual practice, start by letting go of your judgments and resentments. You might consider this easy as compared to joining a monastery, but if you have attempted to try to give up things that reside in your mind, you already know all too well that this isn't an easy task.

If you have attended a meditation retreat for even just one day, you will be asked to leave your distractions, such as phones, laptops, and so on, at home. While spending time on a retreat, you are practicing renunciation on many levels: The longer the retreat, the deeper the practice of letting go that is required. Most residential retreats are set up so that the participant is living the lifestyle of a monastic while there. Each day is completely structured from early morning until you fall asleep at night. All needs are taken care of each day. You have a place to sleep, and meals are prepared. Essentially, you are there to practice meditation; all of the concerns with which the ego tries to distract your attention have been removed.

In day-to-day life, our practice reveals the things we must let go of. As we watch the many distracting thoughts that rise and fall, determined to bring a halt to meditation, sometimes we actually are overcome by restlessness and stop meditating. However, eventually the repetition of our practice reminds us to begin again and again. We then let go, stop listening to our egos, and continue returning to the present moment. In twelve-step recovery we are confronted with our powerlessness right in the beginning. In Step One, we have to admit to our powerlessness over our addictions and any negative behaviors that make our lives unmanageable. On the other side of this admission is complete freedom. What we experience with this complete admission of powerlessness is an insight that provides a spontaneous wisdom: Once we get out of the way, we have all of the power we need.

This is also what happens with renunciation: The more we discard what is unnecessary, the more we begin to realize we have everything we need.

Meditation practice is constantly encouraging us to let go of anything we are hanging on to: This is our path to letting go of suffering. We know how hard it becomes to let go of our cravings and become convinced that if we keep this one thing, it will bring eternal happiness. Mindfulness practice opens our eyes to how much we gradually surrender to renunciation. It has become part of our everyday walk.

Once our spiritual walk begins, we seem to come to a crossroads, and once we choose our path, we instantly know there is no turning back. This surrender and letting go, or renunciation, is going to be necessary to continue our journey. To our friends it might appear as though we are living without some of the so-called luxuries and that our lives have become rather simple. This might appear true when looking at our lifestyles, but inside we realize we have everything we need. The present moment is the absolute provider.

Renunciation isn't about white-knuckling it through the day in the absence of something we know we can't live without, or for some unseen spiritual gift. The practice of renunciation proves again and again that we are choosing to sidestep the ordinary worldly preoccupations. We are choosing instead to walk with God.

CHAPTER FIFTY-NINE

LIVE, LOVE, LAUGH, AND BE HAPPY

The title of this chapter is one of the mantras that have been written on my heart ever since my early recovery. If anyone ever asked my first teacher, Flobird, "What is God's will?", her simple answer would be to "live, love, laugh, and be happy," and certainly to become a channel to give it away to others. We love to confuse the reason why we are on this planet with some esoteric answer that would addle the minds of even the greatest religious scholars, yet our simple path encourages us to lighten up before we look for enlightenment.

The spiritual path requires great discipline that we must adhere to, but in the end it's quite simple: We must serve others with great joy and unconditional love. When we step out of ourselves and become willing to serve others with compassion, we are significantly surprised to see that if we practice this mantra rather than dwell on our own demands or expectations, life continues to guide, heal, and nourish us.

For us to realize the joy of our true nature and to honor God's will each day, it helps to be in a place of contentment and not to constantly search for more activities geared toward personal satisfaction. If we're constantly engaged in planning our next trip, or even what we are going to do in the next few hours, we are creating a diversion and blocking the present moment. There is a direct link between being present, or "nonbeing," and the number of things we grasp at to feel fulfilled. The more we grasp at some experience or outside thing to feel joy, the more we cut off the flow of our true joy that lives within our true nature. The more we are present, the more we are able to let this joy flow freely, and we truly live, love, laugh, and are happy, right here and right now.

We are on this Earth for a definite purpose, and that is to become channels of God's will. But to do so we must reclaim the present moment. This is the highest path to self-realization. After understanding this, we then take on the identity of a spiritual warrior. No matter what career we have been guided to, whether it be a PhD or a trash collector, our real calling is to pick up our flame of love and use it to ignite the spark that awakens others who also seek.

In Chapter Fifty-Five, I talked about the six practices to open our hearts, and joyful exertion was one of the ways. By practicing unconditional love, we eventually experience our joy rising from within. This is our path to living, loving, laughing, and being happy. When I lived with Flobird in my early years of recovery, she told her followers that no matter how we feel, get up off our keisters and help others. We weren't given the privilege of waiting until we felt good enough to go give love. If we wanted to live and not use again, we would have to dive into the trenches and begin giving and serving. We soon found that joy followed us in all of our endeavors. We began to understand that fulfilling our purpose really had nothing to do with how we felt; we constantly had to step out, be vulnerable, and give ourselves away.

Unconsciously, we all know our true nature is divine, joyful, and peaceful, and that it radiates love, but our conscious minds have forgotten this. Our gift to embrace life is our five senses. When we are living mindfully, these senses guide us to our true nature, but when we are still mentally asleep, we fall into the trap of the ego, and our cravings for perfection and happiness again take over. We clutch at anything that is pleasurable to our senses and try to escape the unpleasant.

This desire keeps us entrapped in self-centeredness and suffering. All of our cravings of the outer world for happiness, security, and sensuality are already ours, but we must look within to find the true source. The simplicity to live, love, laugh, and be happy is within our reach at any time, and it is who we have always been. We just need to slow down enough to discover this truth. The bottom line is that we crave bliss, and our soul, or essence, knows itself to be blissful, but the ego tries to distract us from this truth, and we succumb to the temptation of chasing whatever our egos dangle in front of us.

Spiritual warriors must begin each morning with the simple practice of sitting in meditation and allowing the breath to be our anchor. When meditation is over, we move into our daily routine and try to look for ways to put love into action, no matter how we feel, with our only thought being the next breath we take. When we practice unconditional love, thoughts about how we feel soon disappear. Suddenly our energy is derived from the joyful exertion that bubbles up from service, and we find ourselves living, loving, laughing, and being happy. Our presence begins to awaken others. This is God's will for us; this is being a channel.

CHAPTER SIXTY

REVERENCE

What is *reverence?* Reverence is acknowledging the divine essence of every sentient being on our planet and honoring all of life. When you hold your hands in the prayer position and say "Namaste" as a greeting or departing gesture, you are showing reverence. Namaste means "I honor the place in you in which the entire universe dwells. I honor the place in you which is of love, of truth, of light, and of peace." When you are in that place within yourself, and when I am in that place within myself—we are one. Whenever I see beauty, like a sunrise or a sunset, I always "Namaste" the moment.

When we are present, everything becomes holy. The poet and mystic William Blake once wrote, "For every thing that lives is holy, life delights in life." Staying present is the best way to give reverence to all of life. Living the spiritual principles of the Twelve Steps or practicing the Eightfold Path is practicing reverence. Holding the intention to be reverent in each moment is showing compassion to the sacredness of all our experiences and the experiences of others.

If people would practice ongoing reverence, wars would forever cease. Showing cruelty toward people, animals, or the planet would largely disappear. Reverence is a spiritual principle we can consciously practice, and in our doing so it awakens, invites, and facilitates the transition into other spiritual principles that begin to cascade into our daily lives.

When we live without reverence, we live in a war zone. Our lack of caring for others gives birth to negativity, which brings upon each of us a kind of self-imposed curse with each step we take. Others become repelled when they find themselves in our presence. When showing reverence, we are being led by compassion and gentleness. Each step we take is like a light on the path, attracting others to follow in our footsteps.

In turn, we learn and grow by following in the footsteps of those who came before us and following the path lovingly provided by the avatars, mystics, teachers, and all of our spiritual ancestors. Acknowledging strangers you pass on the street with a smile and saying "Namaste," even when whispered silently within, invites reverence into the experience.

The more we practice meditation and the more we live from this breath in this moment, the more we automatically start viewing each experience in our lives as sacred. This breeds reverence, and we look at everything as God. We are then unable to bring harm or hatred to any part of our lives.

In my early recovery, I started to learn this principle and apply it to those who came into my life, especially men who would ask me to sponsor them. At first, it was easy to mentally put people into a certain box or category according to the way I observed them. I found it easy to get close to or sponsor someone who I thought was cool or whom I could be friends with, but I had a hard time with someone whose lifestyle differed significantly from my own. I soon saw that living like this, judging others without equality, was causing me great suffering. It was like having a wall around me; if you weren't what I considered cool, I wouldn't give you the password to enter the fortress I had built around myself.

Once I became more open and accepting of individual differences, and began to have reverence for others, this judgment began to diminish and the walls began to crumble. The practice of reverence began to create an atmosphere of intimacy within me and with the men I sponsored. This intimacy spread to others, and I became close to people within and outside the program.

As you begin to acquire a sense of reverence, you will value your friendships more. The depth of your sacredness will expand in relationship to all of life. *Namaste.*

CHAPTER SIXTY-ONE

NURTURING THE AWAKENING OF SPIRIT

The best way to get through our challenges or the story lines that immediately overpower us when we sit for meditation is to accept and try not to manipulate the moment. We gently return to our breath, which is our anchor to the present moment. The reason we don't want to resort to force is because it leads us back to and lands us in the lap of ego. Ego is behind the scenes and is the award-winning writer, producer, and director of the story line. Applying force is the way of our false self or ego. Our surrender brings us back to the moment where ego has no power.

The more firmly we are grounded in the moment to face the challenges at hand, the less effort is required on our part. We can't reach out to God while we continue to follow the manufactured stories in our minds; divine intervention happens only in The Now. We suddenly notice that The Now is bathed in grace and saturated with love, and there is no room left for self-will; only the acceptance of *what is* remains. Each time we return to the breath, we are giving consent to live in the present moment.

The more we practice surrendering to the moment and what it offers, the more we allow the transformation or the profound personality change to continue, develop, and grow. This is the birth and blossoming of our awakening, and we soon realize that it flowers with the fruits of grace. All we need to do is continue our practice in order to reap the benefits of this harvest. In remembering to remain mindful during our meditation practice, we realize that following the ego is delusion rather than discipline.

It takes great vigilance to follow the terrain mapped out through our meditation practice. The further we travel down the spiritual path, the more we understand that we are always on a journey whose destination is the unknown. Yet as we continue with our habit of showing up each day to participate in our ritual of returning to the breath, we begin to experience the peace of being present, the peace of not fighting with each moment, and the peace of relaxing and finding rest in the present. At times we feel the Presence, and some say it is as though they feel God is living within.

Forgetting the self is one of the hardest things to do. We must call on humility and grace and adhere to a life of service, even though we are only granted freedom one moment at a time. Yet our love for the moment is how our journey continues, and the power of The Now bridges the gap of the false self and our true nature.

We must commit to avoiding entering a battle against any new crises, but rather call on our offering of surrender, since any fight we pursue is only strengthening the false self. Our only course of action is to relax with what is happening, remain still, and remember that this challenge to our serenity is a call to a deeper spiritual practice and an even greater awakening of our spirit. This is the answer to our greatest prayer, which is to be transformed. With my first taste of meditation in 1966, I knew right away what I wanted to be when I grew up: a spiritual seeker. I couldn't rest until I experienced divine union. Since those earliest days, this passion to be lost in love has encouraged a life of spiritual practice.

If we continue to meditate, we will experience many transcendental experiences. However, this is not the purpose of our sitting practice. We actually *cause* suffering if we become attached to having some ethereal vision. Even the allure of enlightenment can become our ultimate attachment. If we can see that when these experiences happen they are purely grace, then they strengthen our awakenings. When we fight against our challenges, they can strengthen our false self. Paradoxically, while we are attaching to these transcendent yet temporary experiences, they are also encouragements and have the ability to align us with the path for continued practice.

Meditation practice is about letting go. This is why we are told to just observe our thoughts and let them come and go. Our temptation is to hold on to the pleasant ones and recoil from anything unpleasant. The *Diamond Sutra* says it all: "Try to develop a mind that does not cling to anything." There is nothing better than resting in the moment and entering a place of deep silence, but if you continue grasping, you will be promptly evicted. Do not be discouraged. You have infinite opportunities for reentry to your divine truth every time that you remember to return to the breath. The simplicity of returning to the breath 10,000 times is what nurtures every single awakening.

CHAPTER SIXTY-TWO

THE SPIRITUAL PATH

The spiritual path probably has as many varieties and manifestations as those who choose to be conscious of it and pursue the spiritual journey. If you ask individual seekers, their definition of what they are experiencing may vary depending upon where they are on the path at that moment in their lives.

I have mentioned previously that if your life is full of paradox, welcome to the spiritual path. Within these pages I have offered that the spiritual path is the portal into the unknown. We often hear that "it's not the destination but the journey that counts." Deepening the paradox, the journey is this moment. There is nowhere to "go" because we are already there.

Devotees on the spiritual path, encompassing countless religions, wisdom traditions, and teachings, are propelled toward one unified goal—truth. Their initial decision and ongoing motivations are ultimately fueled by seeking this truth.

Personally, I have no education in the study of comparative religions, and even if I did choose one to study, I most likely would fail a pop quiz on those teachings. My resume shows only that I've been a simple seeker of enlightenment for more than forty years.

In 1968 I was led to twelve-step recovery, which has remained my primary spiritual path ever since. I have expanded the lines and frequencies of my recovery through seeking the experiential teacher of meditation to continue my education and voyage within.

With every conscious breath I adhere to and come back to, I find the Truth. It is not "over there," and there is no guarantee that it will be revealed during any religious ritual. There aren't any secret doctrines that must be studied in secrecy for countless years. I haven't traveled to the hinterlands for spiritual excavations, although my spiritual adventures have delivered me into many holy places on this planet. These journeys were not a "grail quest," but rather my desire to work with addicts worldwide. In living my life in this way, I have been given many insights along the journey that have shaped my search for truth.

Since the "Ultimate Truth" cannot be found in traditional teachings or be easily explained through language, we look within. I'm not a spiritual teacher, but I am a spiritual seeker. During the time I spent under the tutelage of my first teacher, Flobird, I saw this wordless truth put into action through her constant giving of unconditional love. I believe most of us have glimpsed this truth when lost in the pleasure of service motivated only by the love and joy that bubbles up from deep within. If your path is leading you anywhere, let it be in the right direction. Offer your love to others in every moment.

Ignore your mind when it tries to sell you on some complex spiritual pyramid scheme to guide you toward some unseen reality. This is only the ego leading you into more confusion and convincing you to walk in circles. Believe me, this is not a spiritual stroll! Teachers and teachings can point the way, but our paths are traveled by us alone, and we learn through trial and error. The paradoxes are present to confuse the ego, and at times we do wander in the dark, but please remember that during this momentary darkness the sun always rises again and again.

Our greatest revelations seem to come by surprise. Knowing replaces not knowing as we once again find ourselves blessed with grace. It seems as if grace is never earned or even deserved. Why do some receive it while others don't? It is quite possible that grace is always there, but our openness to receive it fluctuates. I have learned from my decades of being in a twelve-step program that I can't judge anyone's progress. The guy in the gutter may fully awaken in the blink of an eye. It seems like we become more open when we are beaten down, but even that is not a certainty.

My hope is that your journey continues and that you can remain mindful. While on this journey you will meet many people. Your presence will be a gift to others, and their presence will be a gift to you. Do not miss a sacred moment while being distracted by a thought that has kidnapped you. Whatever your ego is dangling in front of you, the offer never lasts for long. So travel onward, touch hearts, relieve suffering, be of service, and carry the message, which has always been the spiritual awakening.

CHAPTER SIXTY-THREE

THE NEVER-ENDING DIALOGUE

A book of this nature should probably never have a chapter entitled "The End." When we write about spiritual matters, our ideas of what that means change again and again. I worked on this book for about two years. As I review some of the previous chapters, I could easily add to them because of new ideas or insights I've gained over the years. In this moment that isn't going to happen, because there would never be an ending, for we are changing with each step we take and each breath we inhale, moment by moment by moment.

The beauty of spiritual practice is that we never come to the place where we suddenly feel it's time to stop, that we have arrived. The longing to experience yet another glimpse of the moment keeps our practice alive. Meditation is something we never perfect. With meditation practice, practice does *not* make us perfect. If anything, it makes us humble. Personally, I keep returning to my willingness to drop all resistance to residing in the present moment, wonderful moment. This seems to be enough. It seems to be everything I need to continue on with the adventure of self-realization.

Challenges and chaos continue to appear, and our practice is not designed to shield us from these uninvited circumstances, but rather to encourage our broken hearts to remain open as we mindfully watch them mend. An open heart and the awakening of spirit seem to walk hand in hand. I believe they are partners that help us all to put our egos out of business. No matter what, we need to keep embracing the moment.

Often this sort of action makes no sense. It's so easy to be convinced that if we could just change this one thing, our lives would be better. We return once again to sitting with no agenda or desire to maneuver ourselves to a better place on the path—we continue to relax and be content with what is.

Return always to your training to become a spiritual warrior. Sooner, rather than later, you will not lose sight of the magic of the present moment. Life is and always has been sacred, and our true nature has always been full of limitless joy. We may not always see this truth, but moment after moment and with each practice, we begin to see this truth with eyes closed and with each breath we take.

The life you are living right now and the person you are right now is the path to enlightenment. Yours is not a life of forced change but rather a life where you continue to show up every day for practice and guidance, a life where the rest will take care of itself automatically. Our path *is* the goal: You can't look at a map and see where you may have started your journey or where the destination is, for the spiritual path is uncharted.

If there is a time for enlightenment, it will always be right now. The next mindful breath you take may cause enlightenment to strike. Now is the time; now is the *only* time. Our future always depends on how we are in the present moment. This is why we are asked to embrace the present moment and what it offers; this way the next moment will unfold as it should. If we are always trying to change what life offers us, we are continuing to act out of self-will. The teachings mean that anything life throws at us is our teacher, even the most horrific situations. Letting go of our animosity and remaining open is what we will continue to work on. May you be safe. May you be happy. May you be healthy. May you live with ease.

I Leave You With These Thoughts

How to become a bodhisattva: Accept what is. Embrace what is. Love what is. Now simply continue to serve others with compassion.

Early morning with the aroma of sandalwood, the monk sitting in robe with hood, gazing with his third-eye sight, views the world engulfed in light.

Don't discount the possibility that the challenge you're facing can open your heart.

Our defects vanish with each conscious breath; while dwelling in the precious moment we are incapable of harmful acts.

As I am sitting and watching my breath, slowly my focus begins to drift to a voyage to the land of make-believe, where I rarely live happily ever after. Gently, I return to conscious breathing. Again, I find peace in the present moment.

The practice of Step Eleven (meditation) is not to become just okay, but to awaken the spirit within and view all experiences with an innocent perspective. Embracing illness or gazing upon a sunset with the same attitude of gratitude takes practice.

When we are practicing unconditional love, our egos will become exhausted while trying to capture our attention.

On a dark, cloudless night, I become lost in space as I stare into the Milky Way. The vastness of the universe brings feelings of insignificance when I am dwelling on my challenges, while at the same time feelings of oneness arise as I see all of life reflected in one star.

Meditation practice doesn't bring us to perfection, but is the continued rebirth of accepting what is.

When we sit with and embrace our own suffering, it suddenly is transformed into compassion for the suffering of others.

We must give, give, and *give*, for it's in loving that we are loved.

Let's have a sit-in where we will watch our breath and travel within.

Meditation isn't about doing nothing; it's about doing nothing else.

Practicing Step Eleven each morning is like stepping out of the flow of time (your busy life) and residing in stillness. Try it; you'll like it.

HELP WANTED: Spiritual warriors to take the vow to assist all sentient beings to bridge the gap between the power of ego and the power of The Now.

The goal of meditation is not to become thoughtless (no thoughts) but thoughtful (think only of serving others).

Hear the sound of an ancient gong echoing off the mountains. Smell the scent of sandalwood as it blows through the temple. Sit and watch your breath, again and again.

Become aware of what you are aware of; this is the simple practice of mindfulness.

When discussing someone's practice, it invariably boils down to his or her frustration with the monkey mind, the mind jumping from one thought to the next. We may feel like we have returned to the breath 10,000 times in one twenty-minute sit. I say congratulations! You are experiencing the practice of mindfulness. Embrace a nonjudgmental awareness of your present-moment experience, and please keep showing up to practice.

Feeling grief and other forms of suffering is inevitable. The arising concern is how we respond to the situation. If we slip into self-pity, we may become anchored in our suffering. Spiritual practice invites us to embrace what the moment offers and lets our hearts be broken wide open. This becomes the birth of compassion, and we learn to touch the suffering of all sentient beings.

As years of recovery gather, our understanding of God may begin to vanish. Find peace within the simplicity that the absence of understanding can illuminate the birth of knowing.

The reason we pay attention to our breath during sitting practice is because it symbolizes the past, present, and future. The last breath is gone, the next one hasn't happened yet, so we can only be mindful of the one happening now.

Practice mindfulness and reclaim what's important in your life: the present moment, wonderful moment.

May you be present for *this moment's experience* rather than trying to change it to what you think it should be.

To look for applause and fulfillment from what we perceive as solid will only result in more restlessness and unhappiness. Leaning into each moment, embrace and accept that nothing is solid or permanent; practicing mindfulness to live more in The Now will introduce us to groundlessness. Moving away from security and stepping into the unknown with each breath is called enlightenment.

Practicing mindful listening enables you to listen to someone else's story instead of your own.

On the streets of Kolkata, a woman approached me with her hands turned palms up, in begging position. My first impulse was to think that she needed to be acknowledged and loved. With hands in prayer position, I addressed her with *Namaste,* and I gently put my hands on her back and said, "I love you." The smile that came across her face changed my life in that moment. I then gave her money before parting, but love is what brought the smile.

No, the universe isn't against you; just breathe and be grateful you're burning off karma.

Enlightenment, or the awakening of the spirit, is accompanied by what can't be described in the written word. Our feeble attempt to communicate the experience would be an eruption of joy and love bubbling up from within. This unconditional love is the essence of what holds the universe together. Yes, this love is our true nature, but when it is experienced at this unfiltered level we know it is pure grace, and we have done nothing to expose ourselves to it. The saying is, "After enlightenment, chop wood, carry water." And I will add, be sure it's someone else's wood you chop or water you carry, for when spirit awakens, we are encouraged to give, give, give and serve others.

A significant challenge has found me; the spiritual work needed to avoid listening to the story line begins. Instead, I will return to what is true. If it weren't supposed to be this way, then it wouldn't be this way. It will all work out in the end; if it hasn't worked out yet, then it's not the end. I'm leaving the door to my heart open to any loving kindness sent my way.

When observing the nature of our minds, we note the way we see things, which enables us to change the way we look at things.

One thing we all have in common once we consciously step upon the spiritual path is the call to let go in each moment. This does not mean we give up, since the only thing we give up by letting go is our suffering. We set positive intentions each day and let them go. Once our intentions are set, if we don't release them, they turn into desire and, inevitably, suffering follows.

When you are awakening early in the morning and are unable to go back to sleep, instead of assuming you have insomnia, a change of perception might let you see you're being called to meditation.

Stepping upon the spiritual path is the beginning of coming out of what we are not.

Mindfulness is a way that we bring the untrained mind into optimal performance, just as physical exercise brings the untrained body to a state of physical fitness. In both cases, it's about continuous practice.

GUIDED MEDITATION

The common way to practice mindfulness meditation is to first find a comfortable position that will keep the spine straight, but not rigid. Some people cross their legs or sit in a lotus position; others find a meditation bench beneficial. Regardless of the technique or seated position, you want to be careful not to cut off or inhibit circulation. If you sit in a chair, be sure your feet are flat on the ground. When you are listening to a guided meditation and you hear the sound of the Tibetan bowl, let this sound be your call to mindfulness, always bringing you back to the breath.

Bring your attention to the breath. Let your breathing be completely natural. Do not force the breath.

During your meditation, the breath will become your anchor to the moment. As you inhale, bring your attention to the nostrils. This is where it might be the most noticeable.

Note the sensation of the breath as it enters the nostrils and feel the air as it enters your lungs.

Feel the sensation as the air gently flows over the hairs in the nostrils.

As you exhale, feel the breath as it leaves the body.

Feel the cool air on the upper lip.

When breathing in, think *in*.

When breathing out, think *out*.

Simply acknowledge your breath going in and going out.

Thoughts will arise; just keep returning
to the sensation of breathing.

Thoughts will come and disappear; observe and do not attach.

When finding yourself lost in thoughts, simply note *thinking*.

If you find yourself judging, do not judge this action;
instead, return to the breath.

Mentally note *breathing in* when breathing in;
mentally note *breathing out* when breathing out.

Do not *think* about the breath. Do not even *visualize* it.
Just be present for the sensations that arise with each unique
breath. Engage in the mindfulness of breathing.

When outside sounds arise, do not go to the sound,
do not seek it out. Let it come to you and pass by.

Noticing a sound as it occurs can
bring you back to the moment.

Sounds and thoughts arise and fall away. Your anchor is your
breath; gently return to the natural flow of your breath.

Just observe thoughts, observe sounds, and observe sensations in the body. Let them come and go naturally.

Let the breathing just happen by itself.

Your awareness simply watches.

The body will breathe by itself.

Your mind will think by itself.

Let your awareness observe the process without being attached.

Gently return to your breath, maybe 10,000 times as you practice.

Let your breathing continue naturally.

Thoughts will arise in the mind.

Sensations will arise in the body.

Simply pay attention; do not attach.

If sensations, such as a pain, arise in the body, gently let your attention go from your breathing to the sensation.

Do not try to fix or alter it; just let your awareness be with it.

Try not to move. If you can sit with it, you will notice it disappearing.

If you have to adjust your position, do it with complete mindfulness.

You might feel an itch somewhere; once again,
let your attention slowly move to this area and just watch it.
Soon it will be gone.

You will notice that body sensations, thoughts, emotions,
and sounds will continue to arise. Our challenge is to bring
our awareness to the moment without trying to change it.

When we notice any attachment to what is rising
and falling, we return to our breath, the anchor to the
present moment, again and again.

Everything that naturally arises will naturally fall away;
we practice watching.

Everything we think about will fall away;
we practice watching.

We observe moment to moment that everything
is naturally and perfectly coming and going.

Our practice is to watch the phenomenon of our
minds and not follow the story line.

Gently returning to our breath again and again,
10,000 times, is our practice.

RESOURCES

Autobiography of a Yogi by Paramahansa Yogananda (Los Angeles, CA: Self-Realization Fellowship, 1998).

Becoming Normal: An Ever-Changing Perspective by Mark Edick (Las Vegas, NV: Central Recovery Press, 2010).

Chi Kung in Recovery: Finding Your Way to a Balanced and Centered Recovery by Gregory S. Pergament (Las Vegas, NV: Central Recovery Press, 2012).

Narcotics Anonymous by Narcotics Anonymous (Chatsworth, CA: Narcotics Anonymous World Service Office, 2008).

The Mindful Addict by Tom Catton (Las Vegas, NV: Central Recovery Press, 2010).

The Neurophysiology of Enlightenment by Robert Keith Wallace (Fairfield, IA: Maharishi University of Management Press, 1986).

The Physiology of Consciousness by Robert Keith Wallace (Fairfield, IA: Maharishi University of Management Press, 1993).

The Power of Now: A Guide to Spiritual Enlightenment by Eckhart Tolle (Novato, CA: New World Library, 2004).

The Tibetan Book of Living and Dying by Sogyal Rinpoche (San Francisco, CA: HarperOne, 2012).

Yoga and the Twelve-Step Path by Kyczy Hawk (Las Vegas, NV: Central Recovery Press, 2012).